South Carolina

South Carolina

R. Conrad Stein

Children's Press®
A Division of Grolier Publishing
New York   London   Hong Kong   Sydney
Danbury, Connecticut

Frontispiece: Harbor Town, Hilton Head

Front cover: Mansions in Charleston

Back cover: Barn with flowers

Consultant: Mary L. Morgan, South Carolina State Library

Please note: All statistics are as up-to-date as possible at the time of publication.

Visit Children's Press on the Internet at http://publishing.grolier.com

Book production by Editorial Directions, Inc.

Library of Congress Cataloging-in-Publication Data

Stein, R. Conrad.
    South Carolina / by R. Conrad Stein.
      144 p. 24 cm. — (America the beautiful. Second series)
    Includes bibliographical references (p.) and index.
    Summary : Describes the geography, plants and animals, history, economy, language, religions, culture, sports and arts, and people of the state of South Carolina.
      ISBN 0-516-20997-3
      1. South Carolina—Juvenile literature. [1. South Carolina.] I. Title. II. Series.
F269.3.S74 1999
975.7—dc21   98-7983
                                                                                                    CIP
                                                                                                    AC

©1999 by Children's Press®, a division of Grolier Publishing Co., Inc.
All rights reserved. Published simultaneously in Canada
Printed in the United States of America
1 2 3 4 5 6 7 8 9 10 R 08 07 06 05 04 03 02 01 00 99

Acknowledgments

The author wishes to thank the South Carolina Department of Parks, Recreation, and Tourism for their help in preparing this book. That department's theme is appropriate for the lovely and friendly Palmetto State: SMILING FACES, BEAUTIFUL PLACES.

Historic homes

Table Rock State Park

Whitewater Falls

Contents

Carolina wren

Myrtle Beach

Greenville

Yorktown at Patriots Point

Brookgreen Gardens

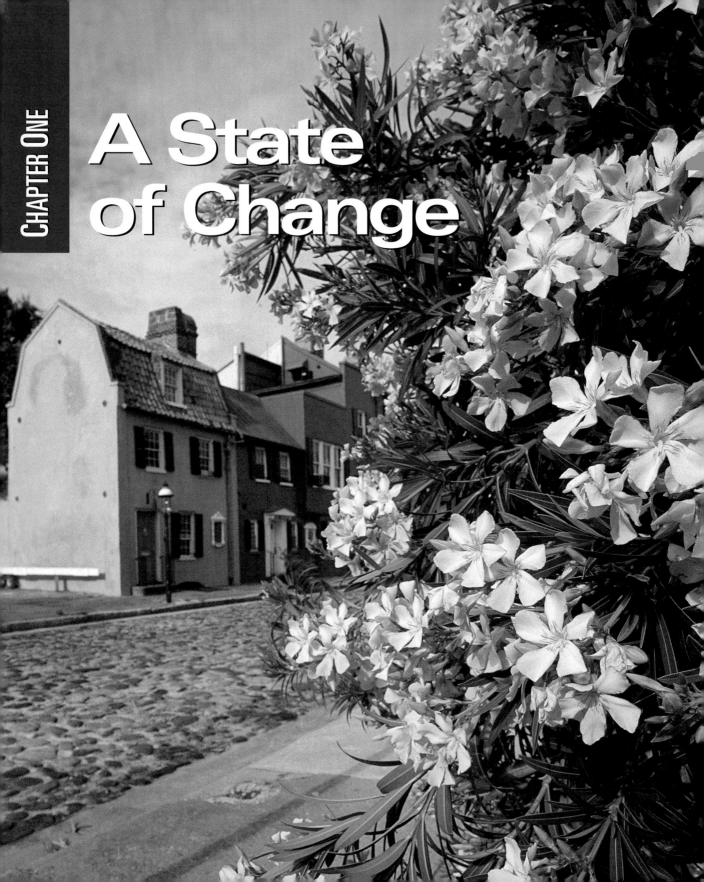

CHAPTER ONE

A State of Change

n May 1997, the people of South Carolina gave ninety-four-year-old Strom Thurmond a special celebration. The occasion? Thurmond had served forty-one years and ten months in the U.S. Senate, making him the longest-standing senator in history.

Thurmond grew up in the town of Edgefield and won his first election in 1932. In 1944, he parachuted on D-Day onto the beaches at Normandy, France, even though he was considered too old to be a combat soldier. He served as governor of South Carolina from 1947 to 1951, and he ran for president of the United States in 1948. Like many South Carolinians of his era, Thurmond had firm convictions on racial segregation. In the 1950s, he said, "We believe that there are not enough troops in the Army to force southern people to accept Negroes into our theaters, swimming pools, and homes." But a few years after that speech he appointed African-Americans to high positions on his staff. He also backed the extension of a voting-rights law. Blacks now vote for him in large numbers. Strom Thurmond accepted change. Change, in fact, is the key to the South Carolina story.

South Carolina is a Deep South state. For generations, its black residents lived as second-class citizens. The state's poor people, white or black, were ill-educated, and many worked as farmers on land they rented and did not own. In the 1950s and 1960s, blacks

Strom Thurmond has served as a U.S. senator longer than any other person in history.

Opposite: Homes on Charleston's Chalmers Street

Geopolitical map of South Carolina

fought the laws that kept them out of restaurants and compelled them to sit in the back seats of buses. South Carolina, to the amazement of the country, led the South in accepting the goals of this struggle. Yes, there were incidents of violence as South Carolina shed itself of old customs and old practices. For the most part, however, the changes came with dignity.

Some aspects of South Carolina life have resisted change, and the state is better for that. South Carolinians conduct their affairs with a certain timeless grace. The idealized image of the "southern gentleman" who displays honor and impeccable manners may have been born in South Carolina. South Carolinians of all walks of life are friendly to neighbors and strangers alike. Perhaps this friendliness blossoms from South Carolina's pleasant and very beautiful land. It is called the Palmetto State, after the palmetto tree, which grows widely in South Carolina. To the east is the windswept Atlantic Ocean shore, loved by millions of vacationers. Beyond the shore is a swampy plain generally called the lowcountry. In the west, the land rises to form hills and mountains. The west is called the upcountry. Over the years, the upcountry and the lowcountry have nurtured two different societies, two distinct personalities on the South Carolina scene.

Change has certainly altered the state's economy. More than 200 years ago, South Carolina was one of the richest of the thirteen colonies. After the Civil War, South Carolina entered a period of economic stagnation. Its people were among the poorest in the nation. Then, starting in the 1970s, a new generation of South Carolina leaders launched aggressive programs aimed at eliminating poverty. By the 1990s, South Carolina had one of the fastest-growing economies of any state in the United States.

South Carolina has a rich but often tragic past. The ugly experience of slavery marred the early chapters of its history. In Decem-

Charleston's old slave market is a reminder of the way life once was in South Carolina.

ber 1860, South Carolina was the first state to secede, or withdraw, from the United States. Four months later, South Carolina troops fired the first shots of the bloody Civil War. South Carolina's story contains the work of heroes as well as villains. And, in recent years, its people have embraced the forces of change.

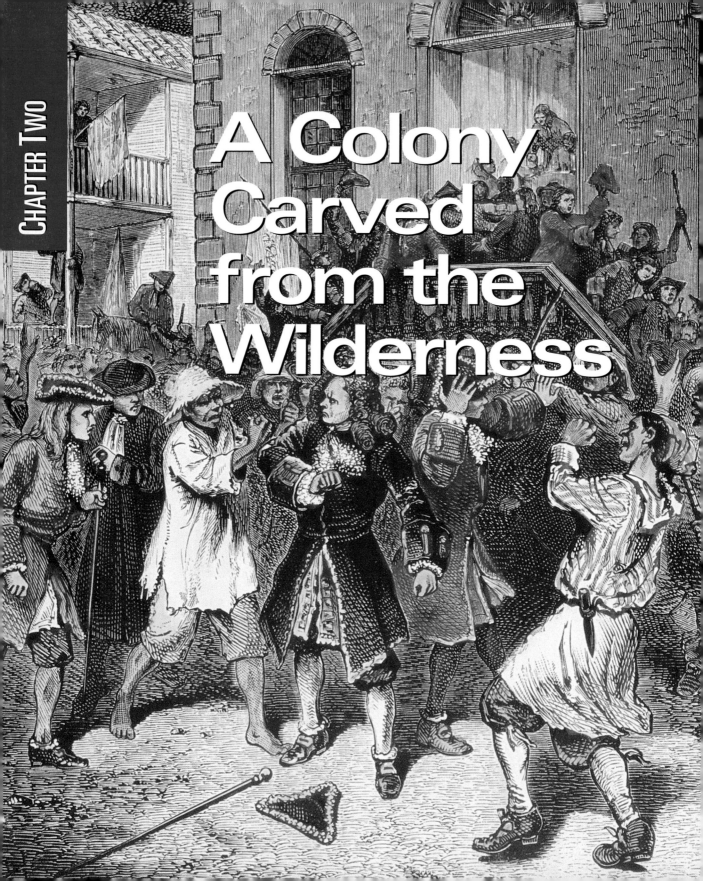

Chapter Two

A Colony Carved from the Wilderness

More than 10,000 years ago, Native American people, migrating from the north, entered what is now South Carolina. They found a land similar in many ways to what it is today. Mountains prevailed in the west and marshes were common in the east. The early Indian settlers hunted deer and fished in the rivers. Those living along the Atlantic coastline and on the sea islands dug for clams and other shellfish. About 2000 B.C., these ancient people began to plant corn and squash. Little is known about their social and religious practices. Their lives changed 3,500 years later in the A.D. 1500s—the "contact period"—when the Indians of North America encountered Europeans for the first time.

Depiction of Native Americans in South Carolina before the European explorers arrived

Life in the Contact Period

Some 15,000 people lived in South Carolina in the 1500s. They belonged to about thirty different Indian tribes. Even then the mountainous upcountry nurtured a different way of life from that of the marshy lowcountry near the Atlantic. In Indian society, the upcountry tribes were the more powerful.

The Cherokee people lived in the upcountry. The Cherokee had at least fifty villages scattered over what is now South Carolina,

Opposite: Election day in Charleston

The Ancient Age Meets the Atomic Age

Near the city of Aiken is a plant constructed by the Atomic Energy Commission. The plant is as modern as tomorrow, but the buildings sit on grounds used as a village by ancient Native Americans. Bits of pottery and stone tools, at least 10,000 years old, have been found at the site of this nuclear facility. ■

North Carolina, Tennessee, northern Georgia, and northern Alabama. Cherokee villages consisted of dome-shaped houses made of sticks and covered with bark. A log council house that held 100 or more people was the focal point of each village. The Cherokee were skilled hunters. Sometimes they used disguise to fool their prey. Wrapped in deerskin, hunters slowly approached a herd of grazing deer. When they were finally within range, they fired their arrows.

The Catawba Cultural Center

Along with Cherokee Indians, the Catawba lived in the upcountry. Though they were never as powerful as the Cherokee, the Catawba are the only South Carolina Indians who still have a strong tribal identity today. Near the upcountry community of Rock Hill stands the Catawba Cultural Center, located in the Catawba Indian Reservation. Guests visiting the center enjoy storytelling and dance and watch potters at work. ■

Among the most prominent of the lowcountry people were the Yamasee, who lived along the South Carolina and Georgia coasts. Their villages were smaller and more scattered than those of the Cherokee. Oysters and clams made up much of the Yamasee diet. The Yamasee people built sturdy dugout canoes and traded with other tribes along the rivers and the Atlantic coast. The Yamasee and all the lowcountry people lived in fear of a small but fierce tribe called the Westo. Warriors of the Westo people ranged up and down the coast and were believed to be cannibals.

Although the South Carolina tribes had distinct cultures, they shared some common traits. Religion dominated their lives. The people believed in a single all-powerful creator and a host of lesser gods and spirits. They delighted in dancing and storytelling. Young men from rival villages played a rough-and-tumble version of football. Games similar to dice were also popular. Each village had skilled craftspeople who fashioned pottery and tools. Though tribal wars were bloody, the people were gracious to strangers. In the years to come, their sense of kindness led them to feed starving Europeans. But waging war weakened their societies. The tribes were unable to unite and fight a new enemy who came by sea. This weakness was exploited by the whites.

Just thirty years after Christopher Columbus's first voyage to the Western Hemisphere, the Spanish sea captain Francisco Gordillo sailed along the South Carolina coast. Gordillo stopped at a coastal village to trade goods. In the course of the trading session, he captured about 150 Indians and took them aboard his ship as slaves. This episode began an unhappy relationship between Indians and whites in South Carolina.

Chicora, the Storytelling Master

While stopping to explore the Carolina coast, Spaniard Francisco Gordillo took Indians captive and brought them to the present-day nation of Haiti. One of the captives became a special friend of the Spaniards and changed his name to Francisco Chicora. *Chicora* was the Indian name for the Carolina coast. Chicora, who must have been a charming storyteller, claimed that giant people lived in his land.

Also living there, he said, were men and women who had long tails that were hard as a rock. The people with tails had to dig a hole in the ground to sit comfortably. These fanciful stories so intrigued the Spaniards that they returned to what is now South Carolina and took Chicora with them. Shortly after he stepped on his home shores, Chicora escaped from his Spanish masters and returned to his tribe. ■

The First African-Americans

Blacks were present at the beginning of the European discovery of the Americas. Historians believe at least one black sailed as a crewman on Columbus's first voyage in 1492. Other blacks marched with the Spaniards when they conquered Mexico in 1520. As far as historians know, the slaves who came to South Carolina with Vásquez de Ayllón in 1526 were the first Africans to set foot on the soil of what would be the United States of America. ■

In 1526, a Spaniard named Vásquez de Ayllón established a colony near what is now the city of Georgetown. Ayllón came ashore with some 500 Spaniards and African slaves. Ayllón's attempt at settlement was a disaster. Diseases struck the colonists, the Indians attacked, and the slaves revolted. The Spaniards sailed away in defeat after just a few months. In 1562, the French tried to start a colony near today's city of Port Royal, but their efforts also failed. The British were latecomers in North American colonization ventures. It was the English, however, who achieved extraordinary success.

English Settlement

The first successful English colony was established at Jamestown, Virginia, in 1607. Thirteen years later, the Puritans sailed from England and founded Plymouth Colony on the coast of Massachusetts. Meanwhile England's King Charles I studied reports about the land

south of Virginia. He named that region *Carolana* (Latin for "Land of Charles"). In 1663, the spelling was changed to *Carolina*.

Three ships carrying 148 colonists approached the Carolina shore in March 1670. The passengers were English settlers who had been living on the island of Barbados in the Caribbean Sea. The colonial party included at least three black slaves. Immediately the people built crude log houses and called their settlement Charles Towne, in honor of the English king. Ten years later they moved a few miles along the coast to a better harbor. This new site eventually became the city of Charleston, the historic heart of the state.

British settlers claimed land in South Carolina as well as other coastal areas.

Exploration of South Carolina

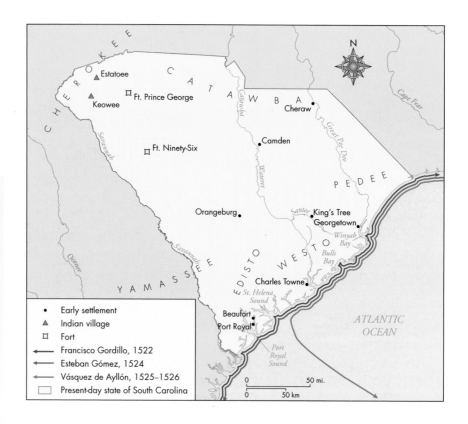

The Lords Proprietors

Each adult male colonist was given 150 acres (61 ha) of free land in Carolina as a reward for making the venture. Women and children were allotted smaller tracts of land. The vast territories of Carolina were given to eight friends of the king. Those eight powerful men were called the Lords Proprietors. They hoped to make a fortune by renting out their lands in Carolina. But as the years progressed, the colonists rebelled against this ownership arrangement. Eventually, the Lords Proprietors lost the land. ■

By 1708, the Carolina colony held more than 8,000 people. Blacks, most of whom were slaves, outnumbered whites. The white population included a large group of French Huguenots, who had journeyed to Carolina seeking religious freedom. The colonists earned their livelihood through farming and through the Indian trade. The Indians provided deerskins and other animal pelts in exchange for European-made cloth, rum, fishhooks, guns, and iron tools. Deerskin hats from the colony became so popular that in England they were called "Carolina caps."

At first the prime crop grown in Carolina was indigo. The indigo plant produced a blue dye that was popular in Europe. Rice

Dr. Henry Woodward, Carolina's First English Settler

The colony's earliest hero was an English surgeon named Henry Woodward. He came with an exploration party in 1664, six years before the main body of colonists arrived. A fearless explorer, Woodward trekked inland and learned many Indian languages. He later organized the lively trade between the English colonists and the Native Americans. Woodward was also the first Carolina farmer to grow rice. ◼

was introduced to the colony by a visiting sea captain in the late 1600s. The English colonists had never seen rice before, but it had been grown for centuries in West Africa. The blacks taught their English masters how to grow rice, and the crop flourished in Carolina.

The early colonists established farms along a strip of land about 10 miles (16 km) from the shoreline. Though the soil was rich, the region was marshy and infested with mosquitoes. Settlers along the coast caught malaria and a host of sicknesses they called "swamp fevers." An old saying went, "Carolina is in the spring a paradise, in the summer a hell, and in the autumn a hospital." Wars with Indians and European rivals added to the dangers of Carolina life. During Queen Anne's War (1702–1713) the colonists fought off French and

Blackbeard was among the many pirates who raided the Carolina coast.

Spanish attacks at Charles Towne. At least 400 colonists lost their lives during the Yamasee War of 1715–1716.

At that time, pirates raided ships along the Carolina coast, terrorizing sailors and passengers. The colony's many coastal islands offered ideal places for a pirate ship to hide and then pounce upon its prey. The most notorious of these pirates was Edward Teach, better known as Blackbeard. He was never seen without three pistols stuck in his belt. Blackbeard stuck long, lighted matches under his hat to frame his face in fire and terrify the crews of ships he wished to capture.

Despite hardships, the Carolina colony grew. By 1721, the population neared 20,000. Coastal towns were established at Beaufort and Georgetown. New settlements such as King's Tree and Orangeburg were founded inland. In 1729, British leaders decided to divide the huge Carolina territory into North Carolina and South Carolina.

Anne Bonney, Dangerous Buccaneer

Not all pirates were men. Anne Bonney grew up as the proper daughter of a Carolina farmer. At age sixteen she ran away with a sailor and began her career as a pirate. It was said she fought with a sword as well as any man could.

Anne Bonney was captured and sentenced to be hanged, but managed to escape. Some stories claim she gave up piracy and lived the rest of her life in Charleston, but her true fate has never been discovered. ■

The Colony of South Carolina

By the mid-1700s, the thirteen colonies stretched along the Atlantic coast from New Hampshire in the north to Georgia in the south. Perhaps the richest of these colonies was South Carolina. South Carolina's wealth and most of its people were concentrated along the coast.

The coastal area's prosperity came from farming and trade. Charleston was one of the finest ports in North America. Every year an estimated 3,000 wagons loaded with rice, indigo, wheat, and tobacco traveled the roads from South Carolina farms to the harbor in Charleston. From there, the farm products were shipped to markets in the other colonies and in Europe. Charleston held 10,000

The Charleston port in 1780

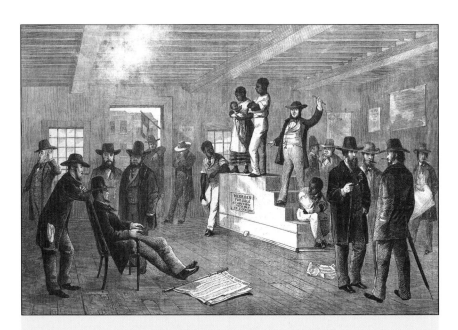

The Charleston Slave Trade

Colonists in Charleston shipped in slaves, many of whom had been recently captured in West Africa. Colonial Charleston was the major slave port for the thirteen colonies. One visitor in 1755 wrote about the excitement caused by a street auction of newly arrived Africans: "There was such pulling and hauling [as to] who should get the good slaves that some of [the buyers] came very nearly to blows." Today, the Slave Mart Museum in Charleston stands on one of the sites where slaves were sold. ■

people, making it the largest city in the southern colonies. The city had several weekly newspapers, a theater, a library, and a museum.

Outside of Charleston, a genteel plantation society thrived. Large South Carolina farms had handsome houses surrounded by lush gardens. The plantation owners were known for their generosity and charming manners. One foreign visitor noted, "The gentlemen in this country are exceedingly civil to strangers, so that a man may go from one plantation to another [and eat and sleep there] and [it will] never cost him a farthing."

By contrast, the upcountry was a raw frontier. The upcountry was connected to the coast only by Indian trails. By the 1750s, white settlers began arriving in the upcountry from northern colonies such as Pennsylvania and New York. Many settlers were Scotch-Irish, a different breed from the lowcountry English people. Fiercely independent small farmers, the upcountry settlers had little need for slaves. This pattern set up an upcountry/lowcountry rivalry that existed in South Carolina until well into the twentieth century.

Whites coming into the upcountry triggered a war with the Cherokee. The war began in 1760, and it demonstrated the ferocity of upcountry pioneers. At a fort called Ninety-Six (so named because it was 96 miles [154 km] from a Cherokee trading post), defenders killed a band of Indian attackers. After the battle one settler wrote, "We now have the pleasure to fatten our dogs with [Cherokee] carcasses."

By 1775, the population of South Carolina numbered some 60,000 whites and 80,000 blacks. The white people were about

Drayton Hall

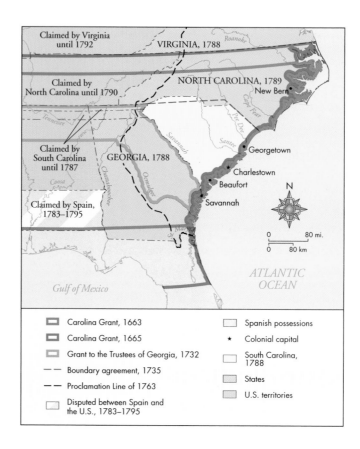

Historical map of South Carolina

Carolina Grant, 1663
Carolina Grant, 1665
Grant to the Trustees of Georgia, 1732
— — Boundary agreement, 1735
— — Proclamation Line of 1763
Disputed between Spain and the U.S., 1783–1795
Spanish possessions
★ Colonial capital
South Carolina, 1788
States
U.S. territories

The Scotch-Irish, Rugged Pioneers

In the 1700s, Scotch-Irish pioneers established farms and villages in some of the wildest and most dangerous lands of North America. The people originated in Scotland, moved to Ireland, and finally immigrated to what would become the United States. Always impoverished, the Scotch-Irish had been mistreated by the British government. Perhaps because of that shabby treatment, they avoided established places and preferred wilderness settlements. The Scotch-Irish were the first to settle the forested areas west of the thirteen colonies. ■

Francis Marion, the "Swamp Fox"

During the American Revolution, a band of South Carolina patriots rallied behind General Francis Marion and raided British outposts in the marshy lowcountry. Marion hated the cruelty of war. Still, he was a brilliant military commander. He led his men through swamps that were so thick the British thought them to be impassable. After directing swift attacks on British units he and his men then melted into the marshes to avoid capture. A British general once said of Marion, "The devil himself could not catch him." His daring raids earned Marion the nickname the "Swamp Fox." ■

equally divided between the upcountry and the lowcountry. Few blacks lived in the upcountry regions.

For 150 years, Great Britain lived in peace with the thirteen colonies. Then, in the 1770s, the people of the thirteen colonies rebelled against British rule. The colonists claimed that the taxes imposed upon them by the British government were unfair. In 1775, shots were fired in Massachusetts between colonists and British soldiers. The Revolutionary War began.

The Cowpens National Battlefield

Near the city of Gaffney lies the Cowpens National Battlefield, the site of an important Revolutionary War battle fought in January 1781. On a grassy field used as a cow pasture, a ragtag group of South Carolinians under General Daniel Morgan clashed with an elite British unit. The battle was a disaster for the British. About 100 British soldiers were killed, and some 800 taken prisoner. Visitors today take walking tours of the battlefield and enjoy a slide show called "Daybreak at Cowpens." ■

The Birth of Columbia

In 1786, South Carolina's leaders chose Columbia as the site of the capital because it was near the state's geographical center. At the time it was just woods and fields. From the beginning, Columbia was a planned city with wide, straight streets. Prob- ably no one dreamed it would eclipse Charleston and become the state's largest city. One of its early visitors was unimpressed. President George Washington stopped there in 1791 and called Columbia, "an uncleared wood with very few houses in it." ■

During the war, 137 battles took place on South Carolina soil. The British army occupied Charleston and controlled most of South Carolina for two years. Not all colonists, however, were in favor of the Revolutionary War. South Carolinians were sharply divided between pro-British and anti-British factions. Many upcountry

The Battle of Kings Mountain was one of the colonists' victories during the Revolutionary War.

people remained loyal to the British throughout the war years. For that reason, an internal war between British loyalists and those who sought independence also raged in South Carolina.

The Revolutionary War lasted eight years. Colonial victories at Kings Mountain (1780) and Cowpens (1781) helped drive British forces from South Carolina. The British evacuated Charleston and most of South Carolina in 1782. One year later the Treaty of Paris officially ended the Revolutionary War and the thirteen colonies became the United States of America.

Statehood

South Carolina became the eighth American state when its representatives signed the U.S. Constitution on May 23, 1788. John Rutledge, a Charleston plantation owner, was the state's first governor. In 1786, most state offices were moved from the old capital, Charleston, to the new capital, Columbia.

John Rutledge

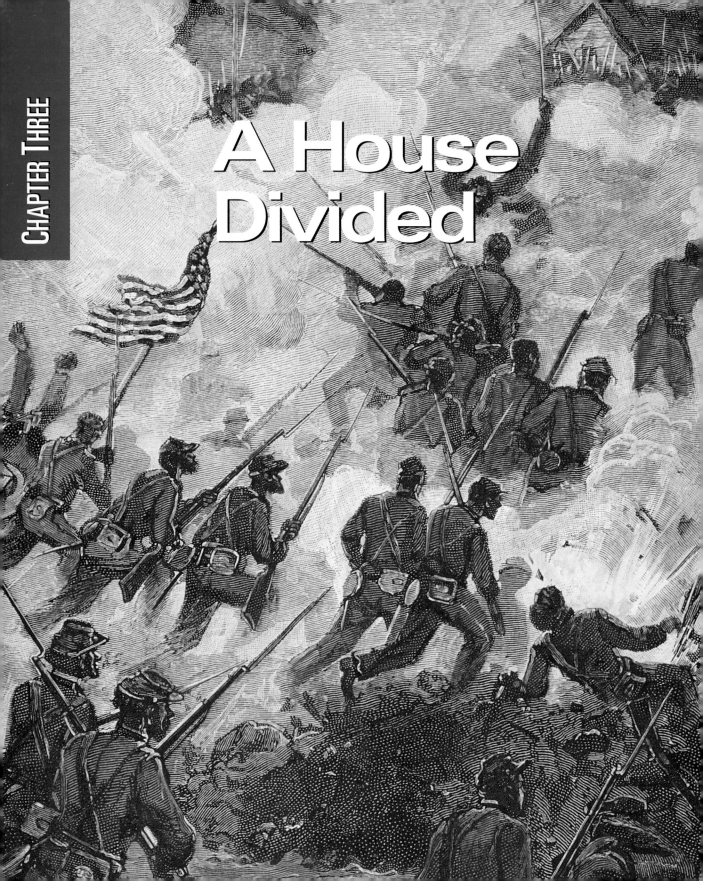

CHAPTER THREE

A House Divided

I n 1858, Abraham Lincoln of Illinois made a famous speech: "A house divided against itself cannot stand. I believe this government cannot endure, permanently half slave and half free." At the time of the speech, slavery had faded in the Northern states, but Southern planters argued that slaves were essential to their livelihood. Even those Southerners who did not own slaves claimed the federal government had no right to interfere with "states rights" and outlaw slavery. Perhaps no other state spoke so passionately for slavery as did South Carolina. Finally, when the arguments exploded into gunfire, South Carolina led the South into the American Civil War (1861–1865).

Picking cotton by hand was backbreaking labor

Prelude

"I'd rather be dead than be a slave on one of those big plantations," a white Southerner told a visitor from the North. Certainly that sentiment was understandable. A slave's life was one of toil, hunger, and fear. Slave children were sent to work in the fields at age ten or twelve. Families of up to ten slaves lived in dirt-floor cabins no larger than a modern one-car garage. Their clothes were little more than rags. Many went barefoot even in winter. The slaves' health was so poor that only about 4 out of 100 lived to the age of sixty.

Still, numerous South Carolina whites insisted they treated

Opposite: The 54th Regiment of Massachusetts attacking Battery Wagner during the Civil War

their slaves like members of their own family. The most important slave in the household was the woman who took care of the master's children. Some slaves were taught skills and became carpenters and masons. But all slaves could expect to be sold at least once in their lives. Being sold meant they would never again see their brothers, sisters, and friends. Slaves on many plantations suffered

The Best Friend of Charleston

Industrial progress came to the state in 1833 when a railroad line opened from Charleston to Aiken. At 136 miles (219 km) it was the longest railroad line in the world. Its engine, called the *Best Friend of Charleston*, caused great excitement. On its first run an army band played, troops fired a cannon, and pretty girls spread flowers on the tracks. ■

The Grimké Sisters

In old South Carolina, it took tremendous courage for a white person to speak out against slavery. Still, a handful of South Carolina whites were outspoken abolitionists—people who wanted to end, or abolish, slavery.

Two sisters from Charleston, Sara (right) and Angelina (left) Grimké, became abolitionists when they were young. Refusing to live in a slave state, the sisters moved to Philadelphia, Pennsylvania. There they worked for the abolitionist cause as well as for women's rights. Sara and Angelina Grimké were among the first women in the United States to become well-known public speakers. ■

harsh punishment if their work disappointed the master. Hagar Brown, an ex-slave from a South Carolina plantation called the Oaks remembered, "Don't do your task, driver will wave that whip, put you over the barrel, beat you so blood run down."

In many lowcountry regions, South Carolina whites were out-numbered by blacks as much as five to one. The lowcountry com-munities lived in fear of slave uprisings. In 1822, the rumor of a planned slave revolt swept Charleston. Authorities arrested Den-mark Vesey, a free black man who owned a carpentry shop. When questioned, some terrified slaves accused others of joining in a con-spiracy organized by Vesey. Even though no actual rebellion had taken place, Charleston whites were in a panic. The sheriff hanged thirty-five blacks, including Denmark Vesey.

John C. Calhoun, a fierce supporter of slavery

In the Northern states, a strong move-ment grew to abolish slavery. Southerners clung to their rights to hold slaves. No one spoke more forcefully for slavery than South Carolina's John C. Calhoun. An Eng-lishman once said that Calhoun argued for slavery with the energy of "a volcano in full force."

Calhoun was born in 1782 in Abbeville, South Car-olina. Over a forty-year political career, he served as vice president, secretary of war, secretary of state, and as a U.S. senator. Calhoun looked upon the U.S. Constitution as a contract the federal government made with the states. He believed that if the federal government violated the terms of that contract, the states were entitled to ignore federal laws within their borders. This contract theory was at the heart of Calhoun's argument when South Carolina struck down a tax law passed by the federal government in 1832. According to Calhoun's reasoning, any effort by the federal government to end slavery violated the Constitution.

John C. Calhoun died in 1850, before the arguments over slavery reached a fever pitch in the United States. The violence of those arguments was seen on the floor of the U.S. Senate in 1856. Charles Sumner, a senator from Massachusetts, made a speech denouncing slavery. The next day, representative Preston Brooks of South Carolina marched up to Sumner brandishing a heavy cane. Brooks repeatedly beat Sumner over the head until the cane broke into small pieces. It was two years before the severely injured Sumner could resume his work in the Senate. Meanwhile, dozens of South Carolinians sent Brooks new canes.

The Whirlwind of War

In November 1860, Abraham Lincoln was elected president. Lincoln opposed slavery, but he was not an abolitionist. He wanted to confine slavery to the Southern states, and he hoped that the practice would die a natural death. Lincoln's leadership was feared in the South, especially in South Carolina. On December 20, 1860, South Carolina became the first state to secede, or withdraw, from the Union. Over the next four months, ten other Southern states also seceded. The Southern states formed a separate government

The Nullification Crisis

In 1828, Congress raised tariffs, or taxes, on goods imported from Europe. The law angered cotton-growers who depended on European trade. Southern leaders called it "the tariff of abominations." Led by John C. Calhoun, South Carolina declared the tariff "null and void" within the state. Finally, Congress lowered the tariffs. But the "Nullification Crisis" divided the country. During the crisis, South Carolina came close to leaving the Union. ■

Free Blacks in South Carolina

By 1860, South Carolina held about 600,000 people. About 57 percent of the population was black. Of those blacks, 9,000 were free. Blacks were allowed to purchase their freedom, and sometimes their freedom was given to them by generous masters. The state's free black community was remarkably lively considering the dismal conditions of other blacks held in slavery. The free men and women organized churches and operated businesses. One free black named Jehu Jones ran a fashionable Charleston hotel that catered mainly to rich whites. The wealthiest free black in the state was William Ellison, who operated a cotton-processing shop. Sadly, Ellison himself owned more than sixty slaves. ■

called the Confederate States of America. This divided the country into two separate nations, each hostile to the other.

Off Charleston Harbor stood Fort Sumter, a federal fort that sat in the heart of the Confederate states. Lincoln sent ships to resupply the fort. Confederate leaders demanded the fort's surrender. On April 15, 1861, South Carolina troops bombarded Fort Sumter with their cannons. All over Charleston, people climbed to the roofs of their houses to watch what looked like a grand fireworks display. The bombardment lasted thirty-four hours before Fort Sumter surrendered. Amazingly, no one was killed. But Fort Sumter was the terrible trigger that started the Civil War.

For four years, the war devastated the nation, taking the lives of more than a half a million soldiers. More people were killed in the Civil War than in any other conflict in U.S. history. In South Carolina, some 63,000 soldiers enlisted and marched for the Confederate cause. About one in four lost their lives.

The bombardment of Fort Sumter and the start of the Civil War

The state's civilian population suffered terribly during the war years. The North's powerful navy blockaded Southern ports. Throughout South Carolina, supplies of food and medicine dropped to dangerously low levels. Northern ships bombarded Charleston, leveling much of the city. In January 1865, General William Tecumseh Sherman of the North led his 40,000-man army on a march from Augusta, Georgia, to Columbia. Sherman was hated and feared in the South because he waged war on civilians as

Union troops occupying the state capitol in Columbia

well as on soldiers. After reaching Columbia, some of Sherman's men got drunk and set fires that destroyed more than half the city.

While the war raged, white South Carolinians lived in terror of slave rebellions. The state passed a law exempting any white man who owned more than twenty slaves from military service. It was supposed that allowing the master to stay home would keep the slaves from rebelling. But as soon as Northern troops drew near, slaves took over plantations. A Northern colonel named

General William T. Sherman led a brutal march through the South.

Thomas Higginson witnessed a group of ex-slaves singing "My Country 'Tis of Thee" and saluting the Union flag as it was raised over a captured plantation near Beaufort. "I never saw anything more electric," Higginson wrote. "Tears were everywhere. Just think of it! The first flag [the slaves] had ever seen which promised anything to their people."

On April 9, 1865, the Civil War ended—a devastating defeat for the Confederates. South Carolina's economy was ruined and its people dispirited. The road to recovery would be long and frustrating.

Aftermath

"[Defeat] is dreadful. I pray God may have mercy on us, for they [the Northerners] have none." So wrote Floride Clemson, a young woman from Pendleton. Most white South Carolinians shared Clemson's fear about the post–Civil War years, a period called Reconstruction.

Many South Carolinians remembered Reconstruction as a time even more painful than the Civil War. The state was overrun by Northerners called carpetbaggers. They were joined by Southern opportunists know as scalawags. Newly freed blacks had the right to vote for the first time in their lives. By 1868, more than half of the members of the state legislature were black. But the state gov-

Francis Cardozo, an Able Leader

Political corruption was so widespread during Reconstruction that at one point a black legislator publicly complained he received a $5 bribe to vote on a bill while his white counterparts got $15. However, a few leaders rose above this atmosphere of thievery. One was Francis Cardozo, a black man born in Charleston and educated in England. Cardozo worked to expand the state's school system. ■

Battery Wagner

At the tip of Morris Island stood a thick-walled Confederate fort called Battery Wagner. The fort could be approached only over an open beach that offered no cover for charging soldiers. In the summer of 1863, a desperate attack on the fort began. Spearheading the assault was the 54th Massachusetts Regiment, which was composed of all-black troops. In a bloody battle, the 54th suffered 40 percent casualties but failed to take the fort.

The courage shown by the men of the 54th, however, proved to Northern leaders that free blacks were willing to fight for the Northern cause. The assault on Battery Wagner was later immortalized in the movie (above) and book *Glory*. ■

Sheldon Church, a Monument to the Destruction of War

Near the city of Yemassee stand the ruins of the Sheldon Church. A graceful church building was erected here in 1753.

Some twenty-five years later, the church was burned by British forces during the Revolutionary War. It was rebuilt only to be destroyed again by Sherman's troops in 1865. Its shell now serves as a haunting reminder of war's waste. ■

ernment was dominated by the white scalawags and carpetbaggers. South Carolinians called Reconstruction the "Rule of Robbers." Government did little to improve roads or fund public schools. Instead, money was wasted on such items as solid gold spittoons for the legislators to spit their tobacco juice into.

By the mid-1870s, South Carolina was near internal war. Bands of armed whites called Red Shirts battled with blacks in the small towns. The hooded Ku Klux Klan made its appearance in the state. Lowcountry planters, accustomed to running state government, quarreled with the scalawags and the carpetbaggers. For several months in 1877, two men claimed the office of governor. Finally U.S. president Rutherford B. Hayes intervened and named Wade Hampton governor of the state. Hampton was a Confederate war hero. More important, Hampton was a Democrat. Most Reconstruction political leaders were Republicans. Hampton ushered in a period of Democratic rule that lasted more than a century.

Wade Hampton

The rise of the Democrats in South Carolina brought an end to the Reconstruction period. Also coming to an end was the political power of blacks. The Democrats found cunning ways—

"Pitchfork" Ben Tillman

Rising in the post-Reconstruction era was a colorful but racist politician named Ben Tillman. A fiery speaker, he claimed to be the champion of poor white farmers. Tillman became governor in 1890 and later was elected to the U.S. Senate. As governor, he likened Democratic primary elections to a private club, and thereby found another way to strip blacks of their voting privileges. On the floor of the U.S. Senate, he made speeches stating that blacks were inferior to whites. Tillman was called "Pitchfork" Ben after a feud he had with President Grover Cleveland. In a fit of anger, Tillman threatened to jab the president with his pitchfork. ■

poll taxes and literacy tests—to keep blacks from voting. By the late 1890s, only one African-American remained in the state legislature. With no blacks in government, laws were written forbidding blacks from riding in the same trains with whites and attending the same schools. Segregationist laws plagued the state for decades.

Despite political upheaval, South Carolina made progress in some areas during the late 1800s. By 1892, at least fifty textile mills in the state made cloth. Most mills operated in the upcountry where rushing rivers produced cheap electrical power. Work in the mills was drudgery and the pay was low. But textiles provided thousands of industrial jobs. Railroad mileage more than doubled between 1877 and 1900. By the turn of the century, about 3,000 miles (4,828 km) of railroad track spread across South Carolina. Farming, however, was a troubled industry. The best farms remained in the hands of a few large landowners, mostly in the low-country. By 1890, more than 60 percent of South Carolina farmers

Mill Towns

The growth of textile and cotton mills in the upcountry led to the development of company-owned villages called "mill towns." In a typical mill town, the company owned the mill, the workers' houses, and the grocery store. It also supported the school system.

Mill towns grew at Lancaster and in Calhoun Falls in the upcountry region. Some mill towns were happy arrangements between workers and owners. Others charged high rents for the houses and high prices at the stores. And they exploited children as workers. An old saying held that management could take advantage of workers all their lives in mill towns because, "the companies owned everything from the grocery stores to the graveyard." ■

were tenant farmers—they rented the land they worked. A tenant farmer was lucky to earn $12 a month.

But the seeds for change were present in South Carolina. The twentieth century saw South Carolina transform itself from a fossilized society to the most exciting state in the South.

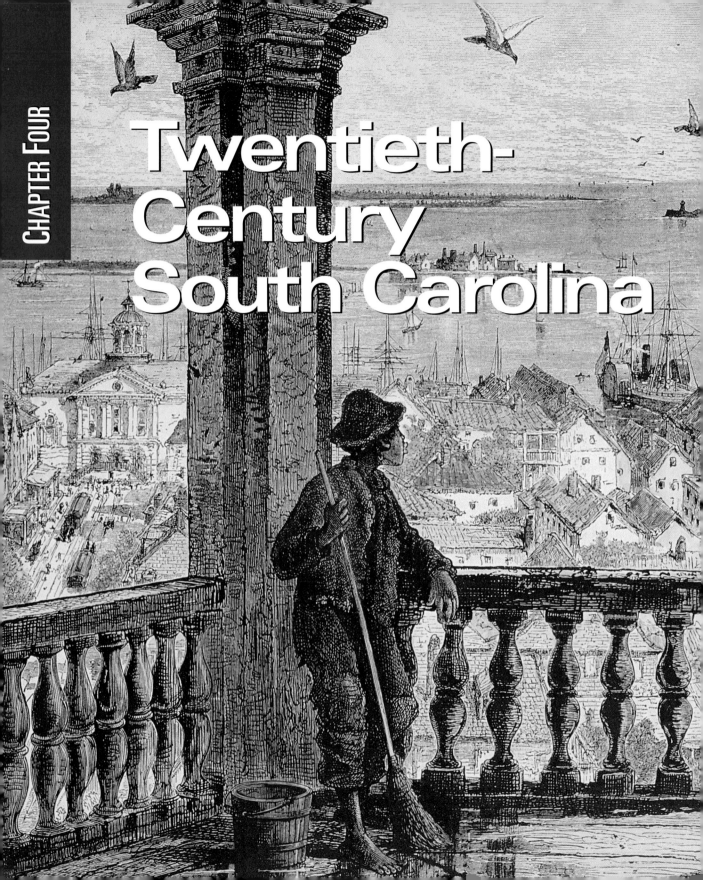

CHAPTER FOUR

Twentieth-Century South Carolina

n 1900, South Carolina was a backward, mostly rural state. Four out of every five residents lived on farms. Its three largest cities—Charleston, Columbia, and Greenville—were small towns by national standards. In states to the north, masses of people were leaving the farms to seek better opportunities in the ever-growing cities. At the turn of the century, South Carolina was lagging far behind the rest of the country.

A Struggling Economy

Agriculture in the state suffered through a painful transition. Cotton replaced rice as the major farm product. But reliance on cotton meant that South Carolina remained largely a one-crop state. Many landowners demanded their tenant farmers raise cotton because it was a nonperishable product—easy to sell. Usually, the landowner took half the profits of the crops grown by the tenant farmer. Early in the century, the price of cotton dropped as low as five cents a pound (0.4 kg). This dismal situation meant a tenant farmer could toil for years and never save the money to buy his own land.

At the start of the twentieth century, South Carolina ran one of the worst school systems in the nation. Classes in most rural areas met in dilapidated one-room schoolhouses and were taught by teachers who had not gone to college. The state maintained sepa-

Some cotton pickers were very young.

Opposite: A view of Charleston and its bay at the turn of the century

rate—but certainly not equal—schools for blacks and whites. In 1907, state government allotted $8 a year per pupil for white schools and $1.57 for black schools. White teachers were paid four times more than black schoolteachers. As a result, about three out of four black adults were unable to read or write.

For South Carolina blacks, the early 1900s were troubled years. Most worked in the lowcountry as tenant farmers. Unlike whites, they could not even dream of leaving the land to take jobs in the textile mills operating in the upcountry. South Carolina textile factories refused to hire black workers. Blacks responded by leaving the state. During World War I (1914–1918), great masses of black South Carolinians migrated to northern cities seeking factory jobs. The 1930 census reported the state's population consisted of 54.3 percent whites and 45.5 percent blacks. This meant whites outnumbered blacks in South Carolina for the first time since long before the Civil War.

A devilish pest called the boll weevil visited South Carolina in the 1920s. The boll weevil is a beetle that lays its eggs on cotton plants. As they grow, the larvae devour the cotton seeds and fiber. In

1921, the boll weevil destroyed half the state's cotton crop. In the long run, however, the boll weevil aided South Carolina's agricultural development. Many discouraged cotton farmers switched to wheat and tobacco, thus ending the state's dependence on cotton.

The boll weevil destroyed much of South Carolina's 1921 cotton crop.

The Great Depression gripped the nation in the 1930s. Banks and businesses closed. Thousands of South Carolina textile workers lost their jobs. Those who remained on factory payrolls saw their wages drop to as low as ten cents an hour. World War II (1939–1945) brought the nation and South Carolina out of the Great Depression. Because of wartime demands, textile mills worked around the clock, farm prices shot up, and new industries came to the state. Approximately 170,000 South Carolina men and 2,500 women served in the armed forces during World War II. The war claimed the lives of 3,423 South Carolinians. Five men from the state were awarded the Congressional Medal of Honor, the nation's highest tribute for bravery.

In both World War I and World War II, thousands of Americans served at military bases in South Carolina. Large Army posts were at Camp Jackson in Columbia, Camp Sevier in Greenville, and Camp Wadsworth in Spartanburg. Marines trained at Parris

Troops at Camp Jackson in June 1942

Island, which is still an important boot camp for the corps. The Charleston Navy Yard was the base for coal-burning destroyers in World War I and—years later—served atomic-powered Polaris submarines.

The Civil Rights Revolution

The signs outside South Carolina restaurants and lunch counters varied. Some said, in bold letters, WHITES ONLY. Others had more subtle wording: WE RESERVE THE RIGHT TO CHOOSE OUR CUSTOMERS. Still other restaurants had no signs at all, but it was understood that black people were not allowed inside.

Such signs were emblems of the Jim Crow South. The words "Jim Crow" came from a musical show popular in the late 1800s. It is a mystery how those words became connected to the segregationist laws practiced in the South. For blacks, Jim Crow laws were agonizing and brought day-by-day humiliation. Public drinking fountains were marked WHITE and COLORED. A small black child who had not yet learned to read had to be pulled away by watchful parents before he or she broke the law and drank from the forbidden "white" fountain. Blacks had to sit behind a "color line" drawn on the floor of a bus. Hotels were segregated. Blacks sat in a separate section at the movie theater, usually in the balcony. Laundries advertised, WE WASH CLOTHES FOR WHITE PEOPLE ONLY.

After World War II, a civil rights revolution shook the Jim Crow society of the South. The revolution began quietly in the courtrooms. Later it was fought in the streets by men and women determined to end the second-class status of black citizens in the land of their birth.

In 1947, Judge J. Waites Waring, from an old Charleston family, ruled on a voting-rights case. For generations, state officials had excluded blacks from voting in primary elections. Judge Waring wrote, "South Carolina is now the only state which conducts a primary election solely for whites. . . . I cannot see where the skies will fall if South Carolina is put in the same class with all other

Three African-Americans registering at the University of South Carolina in 1963.

states." South Carolina blacks won the right to vote in the primaries, but Judge Waring was shunned by his Charleston neighbors even though his family had lived in the city for eight generations.

From Kansas came a court decision that affected every school system in the United States. In 1954, the Supreme Court ruled that maintaining separate schools for whites and

Jesse Jackson, Son of South Carolina

Jesse Jackson is one of the nation's most powerful civil rights activists. He was born in Greenville, South Carolina, in 1941. A one-time assistant to Martin Luther King Jr., Jackson ran for president in 1984 and 1988. Though he has lived most of his adult life in Chicago and Washington, D.C., Jackson has never forgotten his South Carolina roots. ▪

blacks was a violation of the U.S. Constitution. For years the ruling regarding schools was ignored in South Carolina. But when school integration finally came to the state in the 1960s and 1970s, it was accomplished successfully and with little fanfare.

Outside the courtroom, black people took action to end South Carolina's demeaning Jim Crow laws. Most protests against segregationist measures were peaceful. A few, however, were marred by violence. In 1963, a black student named Harvey Gantt attended previously all-white Clemson University in the city of Clemson. It was the first time a South Carolina college was integrated in the twentieth century. Gantt enrolled and attended classes with little public outcry. By contrast, in 1968 black students gathered at the town of Orangeburg to demonstrate against segregation at a local bowling alley. The protests got ugly, state police fired into a crowd, and three students were killed.

The civil rights revolution had astonishing results in South Carolina. Blacks regained their right to vote, the Jim Crow laws vanished, and schools were integrated. Much of this transformation took place over a ten-year period in the 1960s and 1970s. For the most part the revolution achieved its aims without bloodshed. South Carolinians proved, once more, their willingness to accept change.

The New Economy

Before World War II, the South Carolina economy was made up of small farmers and textile mills. There was little heavy industry. Farming methods were crude—mules pulled plows and wagons on most farms. Then, once again, change conquered all in the Palmetto State.

Electrical power is a vital ingredient to industrial expansion. In 1941, the Santee Cooper hydroelectric power plant opened at Pinopolis. Power from that multimillion-dollar generating plant helped fuel industrial expansion during and after World War II. The Santee Cooper project was financed by the federal government. In 1950, the federal government decided to build the huge Savannah River Plant of the Atomic Energy Commission on land near the city of Aiken. From the beginning, the Aiken facility stirred controversy because atomic bombs were made there. However, the plant also employed 8,500 people and brought millions of dollars into the state's economy.

Foreign investment also helped new industries blossom in the state. A typical example is the Hoechst Fibers textile plant near Spartanburg. This sprawling factory, opened in 1967, is a joint U.S. and German operation. The plant employs some 2,200 workers. During the 1970s alone, almost $2 billion of foreign investment funds were spent in South Carolina. Spartanburg County now has more than forty German-owned firms.

The downside of this new investment is that many firms opened factories in South Carolina to take advantage of the comparatively low wages earned by workers. Only 2.3 percent of South Carolina workers belong to labor unions. This is the second-lowest rate of unionization among the fifty states. With few unions to oppose them, employers can pay their workers less than they would be required to pay in heavily unionized states. In the late 1990s,

Peaches are among the state's important crops.

industry expanded at a rapid rate and most workers held jobs. South Carolina, however, continued to finish among the bottom ten of the fifty states in terms of wage earnings.

On the farms, South Carolina found that less is more. Decade by decade, the number of farms dwindled while their production rose. Improved fertilizers and mechanization contributed to farm efficiency. Soybeans, peaches, and tobacco have become major crops. Tenant farming has all but disappeared. Mules were long ago replaced by tractors on the farms. Most South Carolina farm children today have never seen a mule, even though their grandparents probably depended on the animals to pull wagons and plows.

CHAPTER FIVE

A Land of Contrasts

Table Rock State Park
is one of many parks in
the upcountry region.

Travelers agree that South Carolina is one of the prettiest states in the country. But don't look for "typical" South Carolina scenery. Land in the Palmetto State ranges from sea islands and silvery beaches to marshes and forested mountains. This diverse landscape thrills visitors and residents alike.

The Lay of the Land

South Carolina is shaped somewhat like a piece of pie. The broad end of the pie lies along the Atlantic shoreline. At the tip of the pie rise the Blue Ridge Mountains. South Carolina is small, ranking fortieth among the fifty states. The Palmetto State has only two immediate neighbors: North Carolina to the north and west and Georgia to the south.

In conversation, South Carolinians say their state has two distinct areas—the lowcountry near the ocean and the hilly upcountry inland. Geologists, however, add a third region, the Blue Ridge

Opposite: An egret in a
South Carolina marsh

A Land of Contrasts **55**

Mountains, on the western tip of the state. Still, the two land forms—the upcountry and lowcountry—are most noticeable to a traveler.

Take an imaginary trip the length of South Carolina to behold this rich and varied land. Begin your trip on the state's beautiful seacoast. It is a gentle coast of beaches, low-lying islands, and salt-water marshes. The coastal area has thirteen major islands and dozens of smaller outcroppings. The largest island—42 square miles (109 sq km)—is Hilton Head, a well-known vacation spot. Measured in a straight line, the South Carolina coast is about 187 miles (301 km) long, but its many islands and bays give South Carolina some 2,876 miles (4,628 km) of coastline. Also along the seashore are more than 300 miles (483 km) of sandy beaches, the type that lure water lovers.

Inland from the shore spreads the Atlantic Coastal Plain. The plain sprawls over the southeastern two-thirds of the state—the lowcountry. Millions of years ago the ocean covered this region. Today, swamps and wetlands are common here. The land rises gradually from east to west. About 50 miles (80 km) inland runs a belt of forest called the Pine Barrens. Beyond the Pine Barrens are

Hilton Head Vacationland

The island of Hilton Head is named after William Hilton, an English sea captain who claimed the island for Great Britain in 1663. In the early 1800s, it was home to fifteen large plantations. The plantations were destroyed during the Civil War. Today, Hilton Head is a vacationland that caters to people interested in sports. It has more than 20 golf courses and 200 tennis courts. True to its history, the island's resort communities are called "plantations." ■

steep, sandy hills. These hills mark the beach where the Atlantic Ocean lapped the shores in ancient times.

Farther inland is the fall line, named for its rushing rivers and waterfalls. The fall line is the boundary between the upcountry where hills and mountains prevail, and the relatively flat low-country. Most of the upcountry is a geological region called the Piedmont Plateau. Land on the Piedmont is 500 to 1,000 feet (152 to 305 m) above sea level, while land in the lowcountry is near sea level. Continue in a northwesternly direction and you arrive at the

Some Geographic Trivia

The city of Richmond, which is 13 miles (21 km) southeast of Columbia, is the geographic center of South Carolina. In the Sumter National Forest in the northwestern tip of the state stands Ellicott's Rock, named for surveyor Andrew Ellicott. The rock marks the point where the borders of South Carolina, North Carolina, and Georgia meet. ■

Caesars Head State Park

In the Blue Ridge region stands magnificent Sassafras Mountain. At 3,560 feet (1,085 m) above sea level, its peak is the highest point in the state. Caesars Head State Park spreads over much of the mountain. Birdwatchers especially like hiking in the park because the mountain trails enable them to look *down* on hawks, ravens, and other birds. The park's namesake landmark is a distinctive cliff called Caesars Head. Some say the cliff resembles a profile of Julius Caesar, the famous leader of ancient Rome. Others claim the cliff looks like a long-ago dog whose name was Caesar. ■

forest-covered Blue Ridge Mountain region. The Blue Ridge peaks rise dramatically and present some of the most exciting scenery in the state. When seen from a distance, the Blue Ridge slopes do indeed have a bluish tone. The Cherokee called this mountain chain the "Great Blue Hills of God."

Rivers, Lakes, and a (Usually) Gentle Climate

The state's major rivers wind out of the upcountry, rush down the fall line, flow into the lowcountry, and finally empty into the Atlantic Ocean. The largest of these rivers is the Pee Dee. Other major rivers include the Santee, the Broad, and the Saluda. The

Trout fishing on the Saluda River

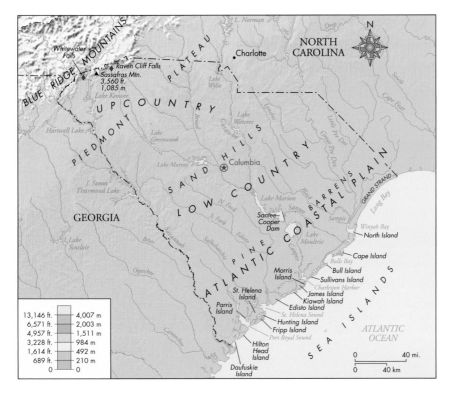

13,146 ft. — 4,007 m
6,571 ft. — 2,003 m
4,957 ft. — 1,511 m
3,228 ft. — 984 m
1,614 ft. — 492 m
689 ft. — 210 m
0 — 0

Savannah marks the border between South Carolina and Georgia. Rivers have influenced industrial development in the state. Years ago, fast-flowing water at the fall line provided a cheap source of electric power. Much of that power went to upcountry textile mills, and to this day the upcountry and the fall-line region are more industrialized than the lowcountry.

You might expect to find the state's mightiest waterfalls along the fall line. However, South Carolina's most majestic falls work their magic in the Blue Ridge Mountain region at the northwestern tip of the state. Issaqueena Falls is a marvelous 200-foot (60-m)-high cascade in the Blue Ridge Mountains. Legend says that an Indian woman named Issaqueena eluded a pursuing enemy band

What's in a Name?

The Pee Dee River was named after an Indian tribe that lived in its valley long ago. But at one time people claimed it was named for Patrick Daly, an adventurous Irish explorer who left his initials, "P. D.," on trees along the riverbanks. Also it is believed that the beautiful Pee Dee River inspired Stephen Foster's song "Swanee River." Think of this and try singing, "Way down upon the Pee Dee River." ■

Naming Lakes to Remember Heroes

Lake Marion and Lake Moultrie are named after South Carolina Revolutionary War heroes. Lake Marion honors Francis Marion, the famous Swamp Fox. Lake Moultrie pays homage to Colonel William Moultrie, who commanded a fort at South Carolina's Sullivan Island during the Revolutionary War. Moultrie won fame for his brilliant defense of the fort when it came under cannon fire from powerful British warships. ■

here. She pretended to jump off the falls but actually hid underneath it. Whitewater Falls and Raven Cliff Falls are two other Blue Ridge cascades that roar over cliffs and put on an astonishing show for visitors. Whitewater Falls descends over six steps, and Raven Cliff Falls is 420 feet (128 m) high.

Whitewater Falls in the Blue Ridge Mountain region

Though South Carolina has plenty of rivers and streams, it has no large natural lakes. The biggest lakes in the state are human-made. The largest is Lake Marion, created by the Santee Cooper Dam, which was completed in 1941. Below Marion is Lake Moultrie, made by the same dam. Marion and Moultrie are connected by a canal. Other human-made lakes include Greenwood, Wylie, Murray, and Wateree.

Generally, South Carolina has a warm climate. Lowcountry regions can be uncomfortably hot and humid during the summer. On the coast, the hot months are made more pleasant by refreshing sea breezes. The upcountry is usually cooler than the lowcountry

South Carolina's Geographical Features

Total area; rank	31,189 sq. mi. (80,780 sq km); 40th
Land; rank	30,111 sq. mi. (77,987 sq km); 40th
Water; rank	1,078 sq. mi. (2,792 sq km); 27th
Inland water; **rank**	1,006 sq. mi. (2,606 sq km); 21st
Coastal water; **rank**	72 sq. mi. (186 sq km); 17th
Geographic center	Richland, 13 miles (21 km) southeast of Columbia
Highest point	Sassafras Mountain, 3,560 feet (1,085 m)
Lowest point	Sea level along the coast
Largest city	Columbia
Longest river	Santee River, 143 miles (230 km)
Population; rank	3,505,707 (1990 census); 25th
Record high temperature	111°F (44°C) at Blackville on September 4, 1925; at Calhoun Falls on September 8, 1925; and at Camden on June 28, 1954
Record low temperature	−20°F (−29°C) at Caesars Head on January 18, 1977
Average July temperature	80°F (27°C)
Average January temperature	45°F (7°C)
Average annual precipitation	48 inches (122 cm)

even in the middle of summer. Winters are mild throughout the state. In January, temperatures average 51°F (11°C) in the lowcountry and 41°F (5°C) in the upcountry. Snow falls in the mountains, but it is rarely seen in other parts of the state. Lakes and rivers almost never freeze over. Rainfall is abundant. Most of the state receives about 48 inches (122 cm) of rain a year, and the mountainous areas get even more.

There are frightening exceptions to this usually pleasant climate. The entire southeastern coast of the United States, including South Carolina, is sometimes ravaged by hurricanes. In September 1989, the skies blackened in midday and winds screamed. Hurri-

The aftermath of Hurricane Hugo in a community near Charleston

cane Hugo, the most violent hurricane to strike the United States in a century, thundered upon the state. Winds reached 135 miles (217 km) per hour. Boats were swept onto the shore and roofs were ripped off houses. The town of McClellanville was almost leveled. Huge trees in the Francis Marion National Forest were flattened as if stepped upon by a giant. Before it subsided, the hurricane killed eighteen people in South Carolina and property damage was set at $5 billion. It was such a powerful event that many South Carolinians think of Hugo as a landmark in their lives. They say, "I started high school the year Hugo came," or "after Hugo I moved away from the coast."

A Wonderful World of Nature

In any study of the state's plant and animal life, it helps to take a geographical approach. Begin at the seacoast and work inland to the mountains.

About 400 species of fish thrive in South Carolina's coastal waters. Dolphin, tuna, sea trout, channel bass, and many other varieties swim offshore. Also seen in coastal waters are sharks and sperm whales. Shellfish, especially shrimps and crabs, are abundant. The sea islands foster a special animal life. Bull, Hunting, and Hilton Head Islands are home to small species of deer, not much bigger than a German shepherd dog. The shores of the sea islands swarm with pelicans, ducks, gulls, and other seabirds.

Loggerhead turtles are an especially interesting example of South Carolina's beach wildlife. The turtles are huge, some of them weighing as much as 400 pounds (181 kg). On summer evenings, the turtles crawl ashore and use their flippers to dig a nest

See the Best of Nature on South Carolina's Public Lands

South Carolina has forty-seven state parks that total 79,000 acres (32,000 ha) of land. More than 7 million people visit the state parks each year. The state also has two national forests: the Francis Marion Forest near Charleston and the Sumter Forest in the upcountry. ■

A loggerhead turtle returning to the water

in the sand. Each turtle lays up to 150 golf-ball-sized eggs. About eight weeks later, the eggs hatch and a race for life begins. Driven by instincts, the baby turtles squirm out of the sand and dash toward the sea. If they fail to reach the water, they will be eaten by raccoons, sea-gulls, or stray dogs. Sadly, the turtles face another enemy in modern times. Some people enjoy driving on beaches, and the weight of their cars crushes the eggs before they hatch.

Inland lie the sprawling wetlands of South Carolina—more than 500,000 acres (202,000 ha) of coastal marshes. That is more swampland than any state except Louisiana. The Congaree Swamp National Monument is an 11,000-acre (4,400-ha) nature reserve where visitors can walk a boardwalk to get close-up looks at turtles, ducks, snakes, and opossums.

South Carolina wetlands harbor fascinating plant life. Cypress trees grow with their root systems pushing out of the water as if the cyprus is standing on its tiptoes. The rare Venus's-flytrap is found in swampland only in South Carolina and North Carolina. The Venus's-flytrap lures insects onto its petals and then closes like a trap to digest its unlucky victim. Pitcher plants and passionflowers bring the wetlands alive with color. Alligators live in the swamps, along with a few black bears.

Edisto Island, Nature's World

Roughly 45 miles (72 km) south of Charleston is Edisto Island, a quiet outpost of nature. Many of South Carolina's sea islands are built up to accommodate tourists. Edisto Island residents long ago rejected such development. There are no hotels or motels on Edisto. However there is a 3-mile (5 km) stretch of beach where visitors swim, fish, and collect shells and fossils. Edisto is named after the Edisto Indians who once lived in the region. People who live on Edisto Island try to preserve their island as the hauntingly beautiful and undisturbed place the Indians once knew. ■

Magnificent live oaks grow in the sandy plains beyond the coast. These are the storybook trees that once graced plantations. Many groves of live oaks are covered with Spanish moss. The grayish-looking Spanish moss is not really a moss at all. Instead it is an aerial plant belonging to the pineapple family. Throughout the lowcountry stand palmetto trees, the state tree. The most prominent tree found in the state is the loblolly pine.

Live oaks covered with Spanish moss grace the walks at Brookgreen Gardens.

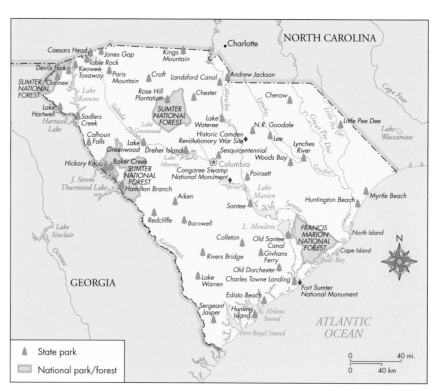

South Carolina's parks

The Francis Beider Forest

The town of Harleyville has the largest remaining virgin stand of bald cypress and tupelo gum trees in the world. Visitors hike 1 mile (1.6 km) along a boardwalk and gaze at giant trees that grow out of streams and pools of water. Some of these trees are more than 1,000 years old. If you stand quietly, you can see alligators here too. The forest is named after Francis Beider, a professional lumberman who insisted that this spectacular 6,000-acre (2,400 ha) forest remain as nature created it.

Rivers and lakes in the lowcountry are popular with fishers. Some seventy species of freshwater fish have been found in South Carolina. Common fish in the streams include bass, bream, crappie, rockfish, and trout. State parks sponsor fishing tournaments for children and families. Anglers spin outrageous fish tales, telling of 30-pound (14-kg) bass hooked in the waters. A record 109-pound (49-kg) blue catfish was pulled out of the Cooper River in March

An early morning start for a fishing tournament on the Santee River

1991. Elderly fishers might follow an old South Carolina ritual. The fisher spits on his bait and then recites the lines:

> *If the wind comes from the north*
> *Fish bite like a horse;*
> *If the wind comes from the south*
> *They bite like a louse. . . .*

Poinsett State Park, a Showcase of Plant Life

Near the city of Wedgefield is Poinsett State Park. Here, upcountry and lowcountry plant life blend together in a rare and curious display. Live oaks covered with Spanish moss stand near steep hillsides that explode with mountain laurel. Nature trails lead guests by streams and waterfalls. ■

The Francis Marion National Forest

Deeper inland are the pine-covered mountains of the Blue Ridge chain. White-tailed deer abound in the forests. Small numbers of wildcats remain in the inland woods. Bears roam the forests along with foxes, rabbits, squirrels, opossums, and raccoons. About two-thirds of South Carolina is forestland. Overall, South Carolina is home to about 450 species of birds. Few other states have such abundant bird life.

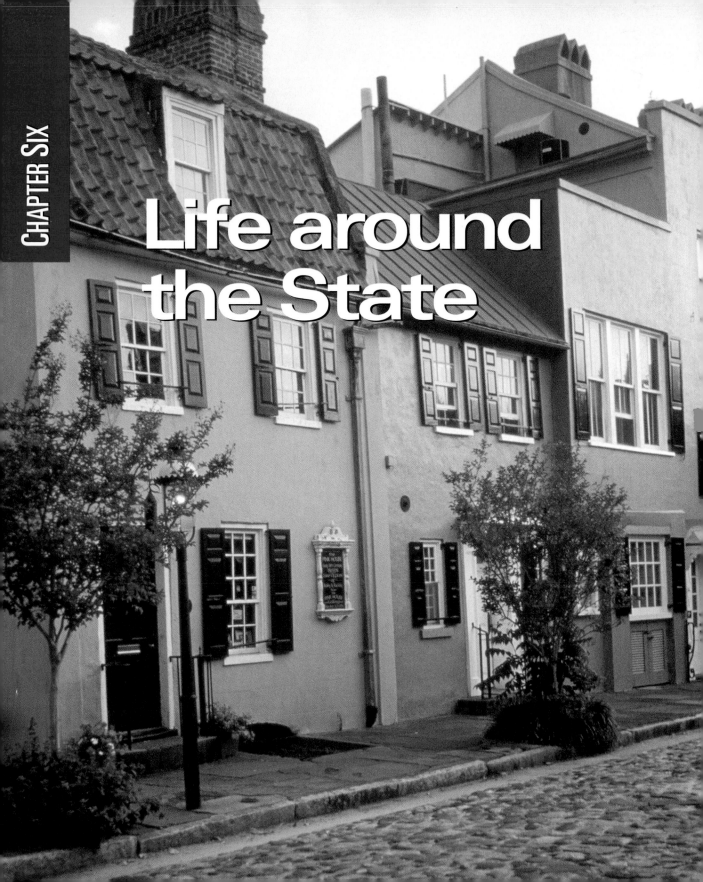

CHAPTER SIX

Life around the State

South Carolina is a land of small towns. With about 100,000 people, Columbia is the state's largest city. And according to the 1990 census, Columbia ranked only 208th in population among cities in the United States. South Carolina has only four cities with more than 50,000 people—Columbia, Charleston, North Charleston, and Greenville. South Carolinians enjoy small-town life, and their communities have a special charm.

Towns on the Coastal Strip

When out-of-staters plan vacations in South Carolina, most study maps of the state's fabulous seacoast. This is sun and surf country. The beaches and islands are a magnet for swimmers, fishers, boaters, and beachcombers. The coast is also where history began in South Carolina. In early colonial times, the vast majority of

Georgetown's Harbor-walk is accented by shops and restaurants.

Opposite: The charm of Charleston

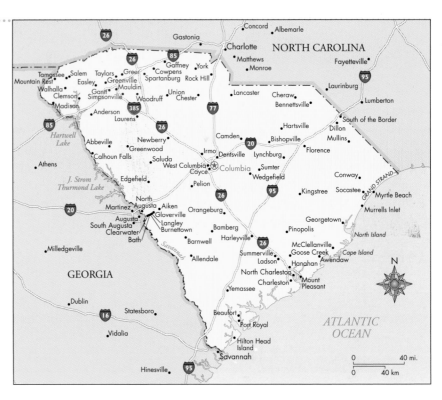

South Carolina's cities and interstates

South Carolinians lived either on the ocean or about 10 miles (16 km) from the shore. Reminders of the past are always present in the coastal region.

Small towns in the state are often clustered in districts. One such district is a coastal vacationland called the Grand Strand. This 60-mile (96-km) stretch along U.S. 17 presents some of the finest beaches in the nation. Grand Strand towns such as Cherry Grove Beach, Ocean Drive Beach, Crescent Beach, and Windy Hill Beach lure surf lovers. Murrels Inlet is a quaint fishing village famed for its seafood restaurants. Myrtle Beach, named after its groves of myrtles, is one of the most popular resorts on the entire Atlantic coast.

Along the Sampit River and Winyah Bay is Georgetown, founded in 1729. In its earliest days, the town shipped rice, indigo, and cotton from its busy port. Today, Georgetown's waterfront buildings have been converted into the Harborwalk, an array of waterfront shops and restaurants. Georgetown's Rice Museum tells the story of that plant's importance to the early colony. Nearby are the villages of McClellanville and Awendaw. Both towns are gateways to Francis Marion National Forest. The forest is a 250,000-acre (101,250-ha) natural reserve designed to preserve South Carolina's coastal woodlands. Hiking and mountain biking are popular activities on the forest grounds.

A summer day at Myrtle Beach

Mount Pleasant, founded in 1680, boasts dozens of pre–Civil War homes. Not to be missed is Mount Pleasant's Hibben House, which dates to 1755. Summerville was once a refuge for people trying to escape the epidemics of deadly malaria that regularly struck Charleston. Summerville's grand old houses and flower gardens have earned it the nickname "the Flowertown in the Pines." North Charleston is the state's third-largest city. It was incorporated in 1972 as an outgrowth of its parent city, Charleston. In recent years, North Charleston's malls and its outlet and discount stores have turned it into a shopper's delight. Major concerts, a circus, and dozens of sporting events are held at the modern 14,000-seat North Charleston Coliseum.

Visitors to Charleston find the very best the South has to offer. A walk along the cobblestone streets of the historic district presents one architectural treasure after another. Charleston boasts 73 build-

Historic homes along Charleston's South Battery

ings built before the Revolutionary War and some 600 others built prior to the 1840s. After the Civil War, Charleston home-owners were too poor to tear down their battered old houses and build new structures. The city's poverty gave rise to an old saying about Charlestonians: "They were too poor to paint and too proud to whitewash." Instead the Charlestonians repaired the old homes the best way they could and hoped for better times. As a result, the city today gives us a grand vista of centuries-old architecture. The Aiken-Rhett Mansion, built in 1817, is a time capsule that takes visitors back to a forgotten age.

The Charleston Museum, founded in 1773, was the first museum established in the United States. In the 1820s, visitors to the Charleston Museum paid twenty-five cents to see what outside banners advertised as THE HEAD OF A NEW ZEALAND CHIEF AND SHOES OF CHINESE LADIES ONLY FOUR INCHES LONG. Today's exhibits cover slavery, plantation life, and the Civil War. Charleston's African-American National Heritage Museum has scattered sites, such as the Slave Mart Museum and the Mcleod Plantation, which illustrate the lives of slaves in the region. Charles Towne Landing, about 3 miles (5 km) from downtown Charleston, is the spot where the first English settlement in South Carolina was built. Visitors today enjoy guided tours of the original 1670 Charles Towne Landing fortification.

The town of Beaufort was established in 1711. Just four years later it was attacked and burned by Yamasee Indians. Today, it is a

Fort Sumter National Monument

At the entrance to Charleston Harbor stands a granite, man-made island that many historians argue is the most important piece of real estate in U.S. history. It is Fort Sumter, where the first shots of the Civil War were fired. Tour groups heading for the fort leave Charleston by boat. Many people who are devoted to U.S. history look upon the ruined fort almost as a religious shrine. ∎

This home in Beaufort was used in the filming of *The Great Santini* and *The Big Chill*.

General Thomas Sumter, Revolutionary War Leader

The City of Sumter and Sumter County are named after General Thomas Sumter. During the Revolutionary War, Sumter was called the Fighting Gamecock because of his dashing attacks on British forces. Fort Sumter was also named in his honor. ■

pleasant coastal town where visitors walk the shady streets of its 300-acre (121 ha) historic district. The Beaufort Museum focuses on the history of the town and its surrounding region. Nearby is Port Royal, an early fishing village. Also nearby is Parris Island, a Marine Corps boot camp. The Parris Island Museum details the history of the island back to French settlements in 1564.

The Midlands, Where Industry and History Blend

The lowcountry beyond the coastal strip is sometimes called South Carolina's midland section. It is defined by its winding rivers, rich farmland, and a growing industrial base. Some of the state's most charming towns lie in the midlands.

On the North Carolina border is a village called South of the Border. South of the Border earned its unusual name because it lies south of the state border, and because its only landmark was a 1950s hotel with the Mexican name "Pedro's." The town of Dillon stands on the Little Pee Dee River. It was founded in the late 1800s by J. W. Dillon, an Irish immigrant who made a fortune in the railroad business. Florence boasts the Air and Missile Museum where ballistic missiles, jet fighters, and space artifacts are on display.

Much of the midlands was cotton country back in the days when South Carolina was mostly a one-crop state. The South Carolina Cotton Museum in Bishopville highlights the cotton crop's influence over the economy. Hartsville once served as a marketing center for cotton farmers. One of Hartsville's founders, David R. Coker, was a scientist who developed high-yield cotton seeds. A flamboyant politician, Ellison D. "Cotton Ed" Smith, lived in

The Mann-Simons Cottage, a Monument to African-American Culture

Before the Civil War began, a Charleston slave named Celia Mann purchased her freedom and made the long walk from Charleston to Columbia. There she made a decision to found the First Calvary Baptist Church. She also purchased a cottage at 1403 Richland Street. The house was later occupied by Bill Simons, an African-American musician and teacher. The Mann-Simons cottage is now a museum holding objects of the early African-American community in Columbia. ▪

Lynchburg. Smith's home, the Tanglewood Plantation, is now a museum showcasing the days when cotton was king.

The recent history of Sumter is identified with the economic history of the modern state. Sumter began as a farming town, and it is now an industrial center. The Sumter County Museum holds relics of the town's agricultural past. Orangeburg too has made the transition from farms to factories. Orangeburg is also home to South Carolina State University, a traditionally black college. On campus, an art gallery features the works of African-American artists, and the stars are on view at the largest planetarium in the state.

Columbia is the state capital and its largest city. Its state house (begun in 1855) is one of the most magnificent state capitols in the nation. The building was still under construction when Northern forces led by General Sherman invaded the city in 1865. Today, bronze stars mark the places where Sherman's cannons struck the outside walls. Columbia's South Carolina State Museum is devoted to South Carolina history and to a vast field of other interests, including laser technology. The Columbia Museum of Art has paintings ranging from the Italian Renaissance (fourteenth through sixteenth centuries) to twentieth-century American art. Antique sil-

Columbia is the state's largest city.

ver and southern folk art are on display at the McKissick Museum on the University of South Carolina campus in Columbia. Also in Columbia is the Woodrow Wilson Boyhood Home, where the twenty-eighth president of the United States grew up.

The city of Aiken is known for its horses and its mansions. Rich grasses combined with an almost year-round growing season have nourished Thoroughbred horses in this region for more than a century. Over the years, fabulously wealthy people have built vacation cottages in Aiken. Some of the "cottages" have as many as ninety rooms. Near Aiken is a cluster of towns: Madison, Gloverville, Langley, Burnettown, Bath, and Clearwater. Many

Breeding Thoroughbred horses has a long history in Aiken.

residents of these towns work in Augusta, Georgia, which lies across the Savannah River.

To the south is Barnwell, with an interesting county museum and a famous sundial. For more than 150 years, Barnwell's unusual vertical sundial has given its people the correct time of day. The town of Allendale was named in 1919 for its postmaster, Paul H. Allen. The postmaster was described by town residents as a "pillar in his church [and] a staunch supporter of all that was good." Bamberg was once a stop on the stagecoach route between Charleston and Columbia. Today, Bamberg attracts people interested in its classic pre–Civil War homes.

The historic Belmont Inn in Abbeville

The Fall Line and the Upcountry

Upcountry South Carolina is a region of mountains and forests. Industries thrive along the fall line, where the upcountry begins. Old towns that focus on their Main Street carry on a close-knit way of life here. And, typical of the Palmetto State, the past is always present in this region.

Abbeville is a historic town of about 6,000 people. Its architecture is the jewel of the upcountry region. The Abbeville Historic District contains many nineteenth-century houses as well as the three-story Opera House. Abbeville boasts that it is "the Birthplace and the Deathbed of the Confederacy." On November 22, 1860, a meeting was held at the Abbeville Town Square urging South Carolina to secede from the Union. Almost five years later, after countless bloody battles, the Confederate War Cabinet held its last meeting near the square on May 2, 1865.

North and east of Columbia is a section called the Olde English District. Towns here were carved out of the forests by Scotch-Irish pioneers. Camden, established in 1732, is the oldest inland city in South Carolina. Cheraw came into being in 1768, Chester was founded in 1755, and York dates to 1757. In a 90-acre (36-ha)

Laurens, Town with a History

The upcountry village of Laurens was named for Henry Laurens, a wealthy Charleston plantation owner. During the Revolutionary War, Henry Laurens was captured and imprisoned by the British. Colonial forces later captured the powerful British general Charles Cornwallis and worked a prisoner exchange: Cornwallis for Laurens. Before releasing Laurens the British made him pay for the meals he had eaten while he was held prisoner.

In 1824, a young Andrew Johnson, who had run away from his North Carolina home after he broke a window, opened a tiny tailor shop in Laurens. Years later, Johnson served as vice president under Abraham Lincoln and became the seventeenth president of the United States when Lincoln was assassinated. ■

park called the Historic Camden Revolutionary War Site, restored cabins show how pioneers and British soldiers lived. The towns in the Olde English District have a traitorous past, however. Most of their long-ago settlers were pro-British and fought the American patriots during the Revolutionary War.

Because of its many factories that make clothing and cloth products, Greenville is called the Textile Capital of the World. City leaders are proud of the Greenville County Museum, which exhibits southern art, and the Greenville Zoo, where more than 200 animals are on display. Also in Greenville is Bob Jones University. The university is home to the Gallery of Sacred Art, which displays biblical antiques and an outstanding collection of religious art.

Spartanburg is a textile mill city with a proud past. It was named after the Spartan Regiment formed in the region in 1776. Five years later the regiment helped defeat the British in the

Battle of Cowpens. Nearby Woodruff has a grand structure called the Price House (built in 1795), which once served as a tavern for stagecoaches.

The lovely Blue Ridge Mountains rise to the north and west. Towns such as Salem and Tamassee welcome visitors to the Sumter National Forest in Blue Ridge country. The community of Walhalla is home to the State Fish Hatchery where rainbow and brook trout are grown and released into the state's streams. Beyond the villages rise the lofty Blue Ridge peaks. Gazing at the peaks a visitor begins to understand why the Cherokees called this range the Great Blue Hills of God.

Opposite: Downtown Greenville

CHAPTER SEVEN

Palmetto State Government

South Carolina is governed by its constitution. The state has had seven constitutions, dating from 1776. The current constitution was written in 1895, and it has been amended, or changed, hundreds of times. The constitution divides state government into three branches: the executive branch (the governor), the legislative branch (made up of the General Assembly), and the judicial branch (the court system). In theory, dividing the government into three parts prevents any one part from accumulating too much power. The federal government of the United States is structured in the same manner.

The interior of the capitol

The Government at Work

The governor is elected to a four-year term. The governor may be reelected but cannot serve more than two terms in a row. As chief executive officer, it is the governor's duty to enforce the laws of the state. The governor is also a key figure in the legislative process. When the governor signs a bill submitted by the General Assembly, the bill becomes a law. If the governor refuses to sign—or vetoes—a bill, it goes back to the General Assembly. There, with a two-thirds

Opposite: The South Carolina State Capitol

vote of all members present, the General Assembly can override the veto and turn the bill into law despite the governor's wishes.

The legislature in South Carolina is called the General Assembly. It consists of two houses: a 46-member senate and a 124-member house of representatives. Senators are elected to four-year terms and representatives serve two-year terms. Members of the General Assembly create new laws and rescind old ones. When

South Carolina's Governors

Name	Party	Term	Name	Party	Term
*John Rutledge	None	1776–1778	Thomas Bennett	Dem.-Rep.	1820–1822
*Rawlins Lowndes	None	1778–1779	John L. Wilson	Dem.-Rep.	1822–1824
John Rutledge	None	1779–1782	Richard I. Manning	Dem.-Rep.	1824–1826
John Mathews	None	1782–1783	John Taylor	Dem.-Rep.	1826–1828
Benjamin Guerard	None	1783–1785	Stephen D. Miller	Dem.	1828–1830
William Moultrie	None	1785–1787	James Hamilton Jr.	Dem.	1830–1832
Thomas Pinckney	None	1787–1789	Robert Y. Hayne	Dem.	1832–1834
Charles Pinckney	None	1789–1792	George McDuffie	Dem.	1834–1836
William Moultrie	Fed.	1792–1794	Pierce M. Butler	Dem.	1836–1838
Arnoldus Vander Horst	Fed.	1794–1796	Patrick Noble	Dem.	1838–1840
Charles Pinckney	Dem.-Rep.	1796–1798	B. K. Henagan	Dem.	1840
Edward Rutledge	Dem.-Rep.	1798–1800	John P. Richardson	Dem.	1840–1842
John Drayton	Dem.-Rep.	1800–1802	James H. Hammond	Dem.	1842–1844
James B. Richardson	Dem.-Rep.	1802–1804	William Aiken	Dem.	1844–1846
Paul Hamilton	Dem.-Rep.	1804–1806	David Johnson	Dem.	1846–1848
Charles Pinckney	Dem.-Rep.	1806–1808	Whitemarsh B. Seabrook	Dem	1848–1850
John Drayton	Dem.-Rep.	1808–1810	John H. Means	Dem.	1850–1852
Henry Middleton	Dem.-Rep.	1810–1812	John L. Manning	Dem.	1852–1854
Joseph Alston	Dem.-Rep.	1812–1814	James H. Adams	Dem.	1854–1856
David R. Williams	Dem.-Rep.	1814–1816	Robert F. W. Allston	Dem.	1856–1858
Andrew Pickens	Dem.-Rep.	1816–1818	William H. Gist	Dem.	1858–1860
John Geddes	Dem.-Rep.	1818–1820	Francis W. Pickens	Dem.	1860–1862

*The chief executive was called president, not governor

both houses agree on a proposed law (called a bill), the bill is sent to the governor for his or her approval.

The judicial branch is headed by the supreme court. The state supreme court has a chief justice and four associate justices, all of whom are elected by the General Assembly. Among its other duties, the supreme court interprets the constitution. The state's highest court has the power to strike out a new law if, in the court's

Name	Party	Term	Name	Party	Term
Milledge L. Bonham	Dem.	1862–1864	Robert A. Cooper	Dem.	1919–1922
Andrew G. Magrath	Dem.	1864–1865	Wilson G. Harvey	Dem.	1922–1923
Benjamin F. Perry	Dem.	1865	Thomas G. McLeod	Dem.	1923–1927
James L. Orr	Dem.	1865–1868	John G. Richards	Dem.	1927–1931
Robert K. Scott	Rep.	1868–1872	Ibra C. Blackwood	Dem.	1931–1935
Franklin J. Moses Jr.	Rep.	1872–1874	Olin D. Johnston	Dem.	1935–1939
Daniel H. Chamberlain	Rep.	1874–1876	Burnet R. Maybank	Dem.	1939–1941
Wade Hampton	Dem.	1876–1879	J. Emile Harley	Dem.	1941–1942
William D. Simpson	Dem.	1879–1880	Richard M. Jefferies	Dem.	1942–1943
Thomas B. Jeter	Dem.	1880	Olin D. Johnston	Dem.	1943–1945
Johnson Hagood	Dem.	1880–1882	Ransome J. Williams	Dem.	1945–1947
Hugh S. Thompson	Dem.	1882–1886	Strom Thurmond	Dem.	1947–1951
John C. Sheppard	Dem.	1886	James F. Byrnes	Dem.	1951–1955
John P. Richardson	Dem.	1886–1890	George B. Timmerman Jr.	Dem.	1955–1959
Benjamin R. Tillman	Dem.	1890–1894	Ernest F. Hollings	Dem.	1959–1963
John G. Evans	Dem.	1894–1897	Donald S. Russell	Dem.	1963–1965
William H. Ellerbe	Dem.	1897–1899	Robert E. McNair	Dem.	1965–1971
Miles B. McSweeney	Dem.	1899–1903	John C. West	Dem.	1971–1975
Duncan C. Heyward	Dem.	1903–1907	James B. Edwards	Rep.	1975–1979
Martin F. Ansel	Dem.	1907–1911	Richard W. Riley	Dem.	1979–1987
Coleman L. Blease	Dem.	1911–1915	Carroll A. Campbell Jr.	Rep.	1987–1995
Charles A. Smith	Dem.	1915	David Beasley	Rep.	1995–1999
Richard I. Manning	Dem.	1915–1919	Jim Hodges	Dem.	1999–

The State Flag and Seal

In 1775, as South Carolina troops began the Revolutionary War against the British, Colonel William Moultrie was asked to design a special flag (above) for the men to carry. Moultrie made the flag light blue to match the color of the uniforms the soldiers wore. He added a silver crescent (shaped like a quarter moon) because most men had such an emblem on their caps. Later he placed a silver palmetto tree in the flag's center. The palmetto tree was especially important because the Sullivan Island fort that Moutrie and his troops defended was made of sturdy palmetto logs.

On the left of the state seal (right) is a picture of a palmetto tree standing tall over an uprooted oak tree. To the right is a figure of Hope holding a laurel branch. The drawing of Hope represents the desire of the state to be free and independent forever. The seal was created in 1776. ■

South Carolina's State Symbols

State flower: Yellow jessamine (also called the Carolina jasmine) This very pretty flower with a delightful fragrance is actually a member of the olive family. It grows in the southern states.

State tree: Palmetto There is still another Revolutionary War legend connected to this tree. It is said that in 1776 the South Carolina cannoneers stationed at Sullivan Island scored a hit on a British warship and set the vessel ablaze. The commander, William Moultrie, commented that the billowing clouds of smoke coming from the ship looked like a fully grown palmetto tree. Thus South Carolina got its nickname as the Palmetto State.

State stone: Blue granite Granite has been mined in South Carolina quarries for many years. South Carolina is among the top ten producers of granite among the fifty states.

State gemstone: Amethyst This gem is a bluish violet variety of quartz often used by jewelers.

State fish: Striped bass They grow big in South Carolina, especially in Lake Murray, and are a popular catch with fishers.

South Carolina's State Song
"Carolina"

Written by Anne Custis Burgess with words by Henry Timrod, "Carolina" was officially adopted as the state song in 1911.

The despot treads thy sacred sands,
Thy pines give shelter to his bands;
Thy sons stand by with idle hands,
Carolina!
He breathes at ease thy airs of balm,
He scorns the lances of thy palm;
Oh! who shall break thy craven calm,
Carolina!
Thy ancient fame is growing dim,
A spot is on thy garment's rim;
Give to the winds thy battle-hymn,
Carolina!

State game bird: Wild turkey This animal was prized by upcountry pioneers. A wild turkey can weigh as much as 20 pounds (9 kg) and provide a feast for families.

State fruit: Peach With more than a million peach trees growing in Edgefield County alone, this choice is a natural one for South Carolina.

State reptile: Loggerhead turtle Thousands of loggerheads live off state beaches, and the state has launched vigorous programs to protect them.

State hospitality beverage: Tea The first state to grow tea and the only state to produce it for business, South Carolina adopted tea as its official hospitality beverage on April 30, 1995.

State bird: Carolina wren Many farm families wake up in the morning to the song of the Carolina wren. For unknown reasons the Carolina wren, which is common in the South, likes to nest on farm buildings. It is the farmer's and gardener's friend because it eats insects.

State animal: White-tailed deer The white-tail is the most common variety of deer in the state. It is found throughout South Carolina, especially in the upcountry pine forests. ■

Kingstree's local courthouse

opinion, it violates the constitution's terms. The judicial department also includes circuit courts and the South Carolina Court of Appeals.

Local government is administered by county and township organizations. Maintaining roads, funding the school system, providing for a police force, and imposing property taxes are important functions of local government. In the early 1990s, South Carolina had 46 counties, 91 school districts, and 270 incorporated townships.

In order to vote in South Carolina, one must be eighteen years of age, a resident of the state for at least thirty days, and a U.S.

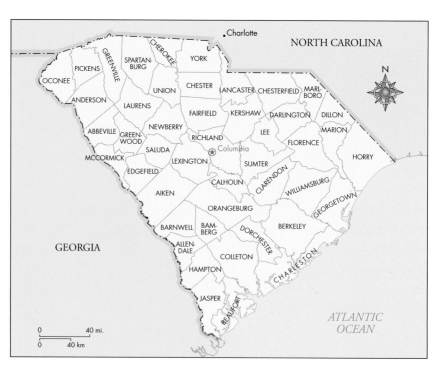

South Carolina's counties

South Carolina's State Government

Executive Branch

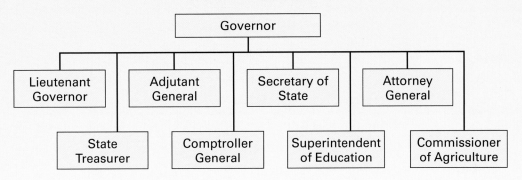

Legislative Branch

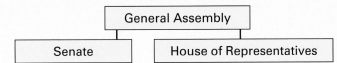

Judicial Branch

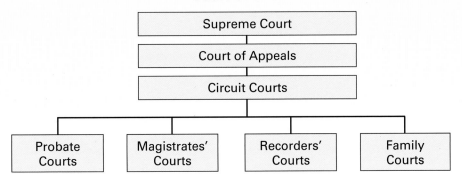

Taxing and Spending

Running state government is an expensive business. In the 1990s, the annual state budget approached $7 billion. Costing almost $3 billion a year, the public school system is the largest single expense. The cost of government is financed through a variety of taxes. South Carolinians pay a state sales tax when they buy goods at stores. Workers pay a state income tax on their wages. Corporations also pay a corporate tax. Special taxes are levied on gasoline, alcohol, and cigarettes. ■

citizen. Officers elected statewide include the governor, the lieutenant governor, the secretary of state, the attorney general, the treasurer, the comptroller general, the secretary of agriculture, and the superintendent of education. All the officers elected on a statewide basis serve four-year terms.

Palmetto Politics

In the political arena, change—much of it taking place in recent years—has been the trend of the Palmetto State. From 1830 until the 1960s, the Democratic Party dominated South Carolina. Many South Carolinians lived their entire lives voting only for Democratic candidates. In 1940, for example, an astonishing 96 percent of South Carolinians voted for Franklin D. Roosevelt, the Democratic candidate for president. Certainly the political situation was different in the past. South Carolina blacks were generally not allowed to vote until well into the 1950s. And there were profound differences between northern and southern Democrats. Still,

Coleman L. "Coley" Blease

Early in the twentieth century, Coley Blease, like many South Carolina politicians, ran for endless reelections, but he was less successful than "Cotton Ed" Smith. Between 1906 and 1938, Blease ran for the U.S. Senate five times (he was elected once) and for governor eight times (he was elected twice). Blease entertained voters with colorful campaigns, in which he employed marching bands led by pretty girls. When he ran for the U.S. Senate in 1924 (and won), his slogan was: "Roll up your sleeves and say what ya please; the man for the office is Cole L. Blease." ■

no other state was so solidly behind the Democratic Party as was South Carolina.

Then, in 1964, South Carolina's powerful senator Strom Thurmond switched from the Democratic Party to the Republican. Since the 1960s, South Carolinians have favored the Republican candidate for president in most elections. In 1979, James Edwards became the state's first Republican governor in almost 100 years. The Republican preference comes despite the fact that the state's black voters, who now vote in large numbers, usually prefer the Democratic Party.

South Carolinians have a tendency to reelect politicians over and over again. Strom Thurmond won his first election in 1932. In 1996—more than sixty years later—Thurmond won reelection to the U.S. Senate. South Carolina's other U.S. senator is Ernest Hollings. Hollings was elected to his first state office in 1948 and later served more than thirty years in the Senate. In the past, South Carolinians have allowed a few political hacks and charlatans to hold office for what seemed like an eternity. Ellison D. "Cotton Ed" Smith was elected to the U.S. Senate in 1908 and remained a senator until his death in 1944. Cotton Ed won largely by denouncing blacks and courting the favor of white bigots.

James Edwards was elected governor in 1979, becoming the first Republican governor of South Carolina in more than one hundred years.

CHAPTER EIGHT

An Expanding Economy

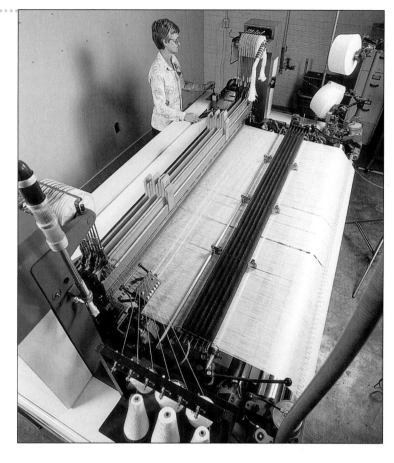

Textile manufacturing has proven to be a growth industry in South Carolina.

Change is the focal point of the South Carolina economy. In colonial times, rice and indigo made South Carolina one of the richest of England's North American provinces. The Civil War, however, left wounds that were agonizingly slow to heal. Dependence on one crop—cotton—stymied agriculture. Industry lagged far behind other states. Then an industrial and agricultural rebirth transformed the state after World War II. Statistics say South Carolina is still one of the poorest of the fifty states, but those statistics are improving. Few other states pursue a more aggressive policy to speed the growth of industries and create jobs.

Manufacturing

Every year, South Carolina's factories manufacture goods worth more than $22 billion. Manufacturing accounts for almost 500,000 jobs within the state. About 25 percent of the total workforce is employed in manufacturing, well above the national rate of 17 percent.

Opposite: Farmers on John's Island

What South Carolina Grows, Manufactures, and Mines

Agriculture	Manufacturing	Mining
Broilers	Chemicals	Granite
Tobacco	Textiles	Limestone
Greenhouse and nursery products	Machinery	
Beef cattle	Paper and paper products	
Eggs	Rubber and plastics products	
Cotton		

Chemicals are the leading product manufactured in South Carolina. Charleston, Greenville, and Spartanburg are major chemical-producing centers. Chemicals made by workers include dyes used to color clothing and other textile products. Textiles are the state's second-leading manufactured product. Year after year, South Carolina is among the top states in the production of cloth products. The state has about 500 major textile mills that make cotton, silk, wool, polyester, and acrylic. Textile mills are concentrated in the Spartanburg-Greenville region, in Anderson, and in Greenwood.

Sonoco Products in Hartsville

The next time you carry groceries from the supermarket to the car, ask yourself a question: who makes those plastic grocery sacks we all use? One of the largest makers of plastic bags is Sonoco Products, which has a huge plant in Hartsville. Sonoco Products began in the 1890s as the Carolina Fiber Company. At first the firm made paper products. Today, it has some 2,000 employees in the sprawling Hartsville plant, and it makes everything from plastic bags to window caulking to motor oil. Sonoco Products, which was born in South Carolina, is a Fortune 500 company—one of the nation's largest businesses. ▪

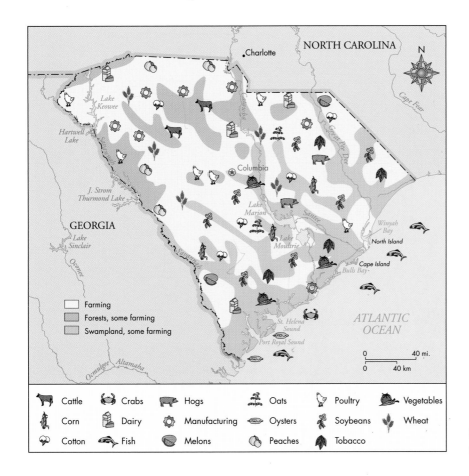

South Carolina's natural resources

The state also produces power tools and textile-making machinery. Heavy machinery is made in the Greenville region. Machinery is the state's third-largest manufactured product. Paper and paper products is the fourth-leading manufacturing enterprise. Large paper factories operate in Greenville and Rock Hill. Other state factories turn out rubber and plastic products, electrical equipment, metal goods, and food products. The Michelin Company has a huge tire-making plant in Greenville.

In downtown Spartanburg at lunchtime you are likely to hear businesspeople talking in German, French, and Japanese. In recent years, many foreign-owned firms have opened textile and other factories in the Spartanburg area. Foreign firms have invested billions of dollars throughout the state since the 1960s. Principal investments have come from Switzerland, Germany, Japan, and the United Kingdom. Two major incentives encourage foreign investment. One, South Carolina has few union members, which means lower wages and fewer work stoppages due to strikes. Two, South Carolina has low corporate taxes. The state government boasts it has the sixth-lowest corporate taxes among the fifty states.

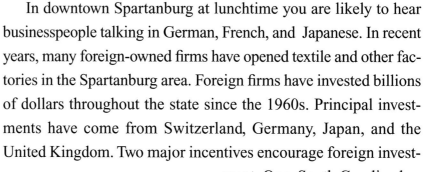

School teaching is one of the many service jobs found in the state.

Other Industries

The majority of South Carolina's workers have service jobs. A service worker performs a service rather than helping to make a product. A bagger at a supermarket is a service worker, as is a bank teller or a schoolteacher. Many service workers are employed in the tourist industry. Tourists spend more than $5 billion a year in South Carolina, creating thousands of jobs in the restaurant, resort, and hotel businesses.

Thousands of service workers hold jobs on or near South Carolina's armed forces bases. Fort Jackson at Columbia is one of the U.S. Army's principal training centers. The air force has bases at Charleston and Sumter. The Charleston Navy Yard remains active, but it has had major personnel cutbacks in recent years. The Parris Island Marine Corps base is still a large recruit-training facility. Overall, the nation's armed forces had more than

U.S. Marines in basic training at Parris Island

Community Cash Stores, a Family Business

Broadus Littlejohn thought he was doing well in the early 1920s when he worked in a grocery store for $75 a month. Then the boss told him business was bad and he would have to take a $25 pay cut. "No thanks," said Mr. Littlejohn. So he opened his own store on Broad Street in Spartanburg. Mr. Littlejohn had grown up on a tenant farm, so he granted credit to cash-starved farmers in the area. The business thrived and expanded into a chain called Community Cash Stores. Today, the chain has twenty-one stores in South Carolina and about 750 employees. The headquarters for Community Cash Stores remains in Spartanburg. ■

56,000 military and defense personnel stationed in South Carolina in the early 1990s.

Transportation is a key factor in a vibrant state economy. Modern roads, railroads, airfields, and shipping docks help farms and industrial plants serve their customers. South Carolina's location is also a plus. Some 78 percent of the total U.S. population lives within 1,000 miles (1,609 km) of South Carolina's borders. Within the state are 64,000 miles (102,976 km) of toll-free highways and 2,500 miles (4,023 km) of railroad track. Seven major airlines average 500 stops a day at South Carolina's airports. The biggest airports serve Columbia, Charleston, and the Greenville-Spartanburg area. Each year, 1,500 oceangoing ships from 120 nations dock at Charleston Harbor. Other major harbors are at Georgetown and Port Royal.

More than 66,000 South Carolinians work in banking, real estate, and insurance. South Carolina has 77 commercial banks with more than 800 branches. Each year, banks within the state handle more than $26 billion. Some 135 newspapers, including 20 dailies, are published in the state. The largest daily papers are the *Post and Courier* of Charleston, the *State* of Columbia, and the *Spartanburg Herald Journal*. About 185 radio stations and thirty-five TV stations operate in South Carolina.

Agriculture and Natural Resources

South Carolina has about 24,500 farms. The average size of a farm within the state is 212 acres (86 ha). Cotton was once the king of South Carolina agriculture. Today, tobacco is the most profitable crop grown in the state. Most tobacco farms are found in the

Shrimp Perlou

This is the main rice dish of South Carolina and the most famous. It can be made with shrimp, which is a product of South Carolina, or you can substitute sausage, chicken, or any other meat.

Ingredients:

1 lb. uncooked medium-sized shrimp

3 cups water

2 tablespoons liquid crab or seafood boil seasoning

1 onion, chopped

3 cloves garlic, minced

3 tomatoes, chopped

3 slices bacon

1 cup long-grain white rice

salt and ground black pepper to taste

Directions:

Peel shrimp, carefully remove the central veins, and rinse in cold water. Put the shells to one side.

Pour the water into a pot, add the shells and crab boil seasoning, and bring to a boil. Reduce heat and simmer for 15 minutes. Strain the water through a sieve into a bowl and set aside. This is shrimp stock. You will need about two cups. Add the tomatoes, salt, and pepper.

In a heavy skillet over medium heat, cook the bacon until crisp. Place the bacon on paper towels to drain. Add the onion, garlic, and rice to the bacon grease in the skillet and cook, stirring constantly, until all the ingredients are coated with the grease and the rice is beginning to turn opaque. This should take 3 to 5 minutes.

Add the shrimp stock and tomato mixture to the skillet and bring to a boil over medium heat, then reduce the heat to low, cover, and simmer until the liquid is nearly absorbed. This should take about 20 to 30 minutes.

Stir in the shrimp, cover, and cook until the shrimp turn pink and the liquid is fully absorbed. This will take about 5 to 8 minutes.

Crumble bacon over the top, and serve.

Serves 4–6

Tobacco is South Carolina's most profitable crop.

northeast, along the Pee Dee River. Generally, the lowcountry has the state's most productive farmland. After tobacco, state farmers grow soybeans, corn, wheat, cotton, and peaches. South Carolina leads all other states in the production of peaches. Cotton, once king, now ranks fifth in importance among the crops grown in South Carolina.

More than half a million cattle are raised on South Carolina farms. Dairy farmers tend to some 33,000 milk cows. Poultry farmers produce annual yields of 1.4 billion eggs, 415 million pounds

(188 million kg) of chicken, and 178.2 million pounds (81 million kg) of turkey. About 400,000 hogs are raised in the state.

Commercial fishing is restricted to shellfish and saltwater fish caught in the ocean. The catch consists mainly of crabs, shrimp, oysters, and clams. South Carolina's commercial fish companies earn a total of about $29 million each year. Mining is not a major enterprise in South Carolina. Leading mineral products include granite, limestone, and cement. Mining accounts for less than 1 percent of the total income of the state.

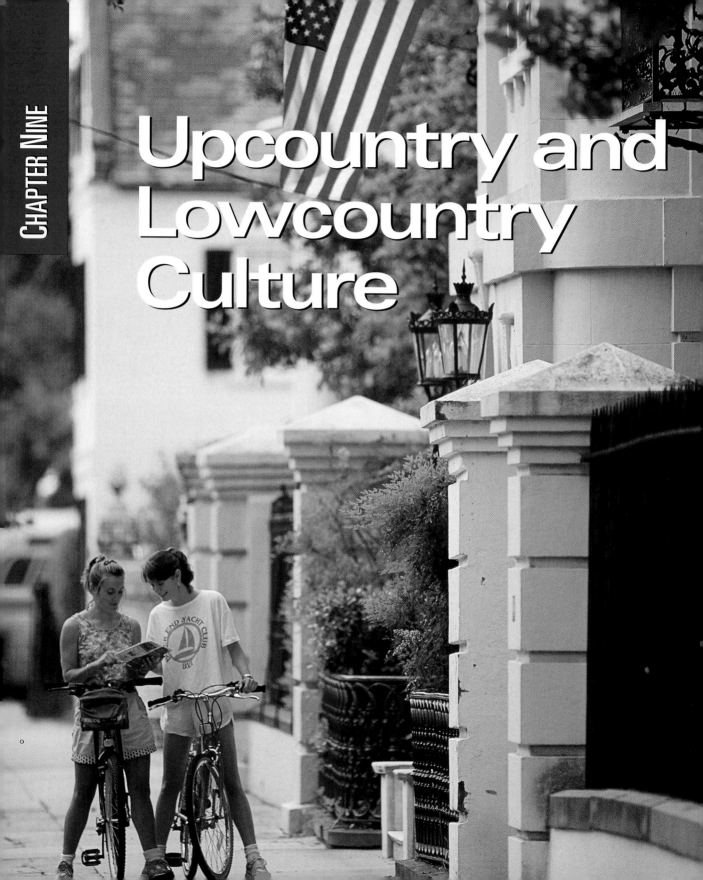

CHAPTER NINE

Upcountry and Lowcountry Culture

South Carolinians are outgoing and friendly. On the street they say "Hi!" with a big smile. The Palmetto people are also hardworking and fiercely loyal to South Carolina. A state's true strength lies in its people. It is no wonder that South Carolina looks forward to such a bright future.

Population Trends

The 1990 census counted 3,505,707 people living in South Carolina. This number ranked South Carolina twenty-fifth among the fifty states in terms of population. The population had grown by 12 percent in the 1980s, and a similar growth rate is expected in the 1990s. People moving into South Carolina account for the increase. Retirees come to live in the mild climate, and young families move to South Carolina to take advantage of the growing job market.

Through most of the twentieth century, the majority of South Carolinians lived in farm areas, thereby going against a national trend for people to move into cities. In 1920, census figures held that 51.2 percent of United States residents were city dwellers, but only 17.5 percent of South Carolinians lived in urban areas at that time. It was not until 1980 that a majority—54 percent—of South Carolinians resided in cities or towns.

The population of the state is concentrated in three main regions: Charleston (which includes North Charleston), Columbia, and the Greenville-Spartanburg region. The southwestern part of

Many South Carolinians are known for their outgoing personalities.

Opposite: Bicycling in Charleston

South Carolina's Population Growth Since 1940

1940	1,899,804
1950	2,117,027
1960	2,382,594
1970	2,590,713
1980	3,122,814
1990	3,505,707

Population of South Carolina's Major Cities (1990)

Columbia	98,052
Charleston	80,414
North Charleston	70,218
Greenville	58,282
Spartanburg	43,467
Sumter	41,943

the state is thinly populated. South Carolina's population density in 1990 was 113 people per square mile (43 per sq km). Neighboring North Carolina's density in 1990 was 126 people per square mile, and Georgia averaged 110 people per square mile.

Who Are the South Carolinians?

Despite a rather large influx of people in recent years, South Carolina's population is composed mainly of people, black and white, who have long family histories in the state. The 1990 census reported that only 1.4 percent of South Carolina's residents were born in countries other than the United States. About 30 percent of South Carolinians are black. The whites are primarily of northern European stock. Some 8,000 South Carolinians are of Native American heritage.

South Carolinians speak with a southern drawl. For example, many people say "hit" for "it." Some older residents use double-word expressions such as "tooth dentist" or "widow woman." Within the state, there is also a Charleston versus an upcountry accent. A Charleston resident, so say South Carolinians, will sing out a word, making "date" sound like *day-uht*. Both North Carolina and South Carolina have towns named Beaufort. But in South Carolina the town is called BEW-fort, whereas North Carolinians pronounce the name of their city BOH-fort.

South Carolina has always been predominantly Protestant. Baptists are the largest single group. Other major denominations include African Methodist Episcopalian, United Methodist, and Presbyterian. Roman Catholics within the state number about 80,000, and there are about 8,500 Jews. South Carolinians, espe-

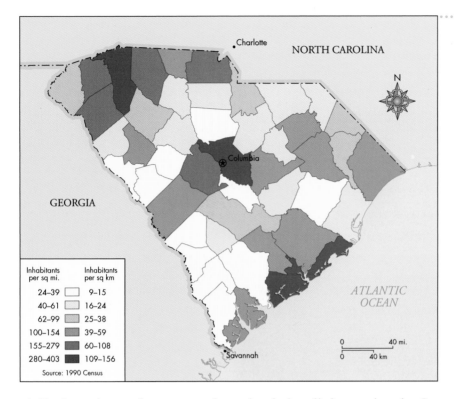

Map labels:
- Charlotte
- NORTH CAROLINA
- N
- Columbia
- GEORGIA
- ATLANTIC OCEAN
- Savannah

Inhabitants per sq mi.	Inhabitants per sq km
24–39	9–15
40–61	16–24
62–99	25–38
100–154	39–59
155–279	60–108
280–403	109–156

Source: 1990 Census

0   40 mi.
0   40 km

South Carolina's population density

cially those in rural areas, tend to take their religion seriously. On Sundays, church meetings in farming towns rock with spirituals and fervent prayer.

Schools

State law says that South Carolina's children must attend school from age five through age sixteen. The state has about 500,000 grade-school students, 90,000 high-school students, and 40,000 grade- and high-school teachers. Maintaining this large school system is expensive. It costs taxpayers an average of $3,700 per year to educate each student.

Beginning in the 1970s, South Carolina launched a broad program of educational reform. Programs for exceptional students were established and funds for the school system were increased.

The Gullahs, South Carolina's Unique Culture

For many years, tiny Fripp Island, St. Helena's Island, and nearby coastal regions were cut off from mainstream South Carolina. As a result, a small group of blacks, generally called the Gullahs, were able to preserve their culture. The Gullahs came from what is now Sierra Leone in West Africa. They told stories that originated in Africa. They developed their own music and their own rice and fish dishes, and they wove grass baskets that were both sturdy and colorful. Most notable was their language—a mixture of contemporary English, older English, and African terms. In Gullah speech, the word "um" was used for *it*, *her*, *him*, or *them*. Because of improved roads and bridges this coastal region is no longer cut off from the rest of the state. Now only the very old people use Gullah expressions and remember the old stories. Still, the town of Beaufort proudly holds the Gullah Cultural Festival every year in late May. ◼

The effort has reaped rewards with better performances on tests. Most high-school students throughout the nation must take SAT tests that measure their eligibility to enter college. In recent years, SAT scores for South Carolina's high-school students have increased by forty points, while national scores on the same test went up by only nine points. Today, almost 70 percent of South Carolinian adults are high-school graduates, and 16 percent have attended college.

South Carolina has thirty-four- public and twenty-eight private colleges. The state's largest colleges are the University of South Carolina in Columbia, Clemson University in Clemson, and the

The University of South Carolina was founded in 1801.

The Citadel

Founded in 1842, the Citadel in Charleston is a famous military college. Books and movies have been written about student life at the Citadel. The college day begins as students assemble on a courtyard with a red-and-white checkerboard design. Surprise white-gloved inspections and hours of marching are part of the students' routine. Over the years, the Citadel was known for its reluctance to accept black students and, later, female students. But, like so many other elements of South Carolina, change has come to the Citadel. Black and female students may now enroll at the college. ■

Medical University of South Carolina in Charleston. Bob Jones University in Greenville has an enrollment of more than 5,000 students and is the largest fundamentalist Christian school in the United States.

Libraries are almost as important as schools in enhancing public education. South Carolina libraries hold almost 6 million books. The state has achieved two important "firsts" in library development. South Carolina had the first publicly supported library (opened at Charleston in 1698) in the thirteen colonies. In 1840, the University of South Carolina, then in Charleston, built the first separate college library building. The first public museum to open in the United States is the Charleston Museum, founded in 1773.

CHAPTER TEN

Arts, Sports, Fairs, and Fun

Years ago it was said that South Carolina was the only southern state that did not have to stand in awe of Virginia. The old saying meant that South Carolina and Virginia were the two states in the south that had achieved the highest standards in art, literature, and culture. Today, most people agree South Carolina's achievements in arts and graceful living rival not only Virginia, but any other state, North or South.

Dogwoods and azaleas in bloom at Edisto Memorial Gardens

Gardens and Plantations

Gardens grow lush and thick under South Carolina's gentle climate and sunny skies. Over the years, South Carolinians have elevated gardening to an art form. The state's famous gardens are among its most popular tourist attractions.

Cypress Gardens near Charleston is a 160-acre (65-ha) blackwater swamp. A wonderland of cypress trees push out of its watery floor. Visitors hike paths or paddle canoes to see azaleas, camellias, and other flowers exploding in color. Nearby is Magnolia Gardens where more than 500 varieties of flowers grow. Also in the Charleston area is Middleton Place, famous for its roses and

Opposite: Boaters on Cypress Gardens

Brookgreen Gardens boasts the largest outdoor collection of sculpture in the country.

magnolias. Dating to 1741, Middleton Place is the United States' oldest formal gardens.

Orangeburg is the site of the Edisto Memorial Gardens. Visitors at Edisto walk paths flanked by masses of roses, wisteria, and other favorite flowers of the Old South. North of Georgetown is Brookgreen Gardens, built on a former rice plantation. In addition to a colorful floral display, Brookgreen Gardens is home to more than 350 pieces of sculpture. Its leaflets say Brookgreen has the largest outdoor sculpture exhibit in the United States.

Plantations celebrate the grace and elegance of the Old South. Many plantation buildings were destroyed during the Civil War. Others fell into ruin in the poverty-stricken postwar years. But several plantations and their manor houses stood the test of war and time. They have been lovingly restored and now greet thousands of visitors each day. Like old structures anywhere, these buildings have individual personalities, and they have stories to tell.

Joel Roberts Poinsett, Statesman and Gardener

Born to a wealthy Charleston family in 1779, Joel Roberts Poinsett dabbled in politics and in gardening. He was appointed the first U.S. ambassador to Mexico in 1825. In that country he became intrigued by a pleasant winter-blooming flower. He brought the flower back to the United Sates where people used it to brighten up homes during the Christmas season. Eventually, the plant was named the poinsettia in honor of Joel Roberts Poinsett of South Carolina. ■

Near Charleston is Boone Hall. In 1681, this land was granted to Major John Boone, one of South Carolina's first settlers. A magnificent stand of live oaks line the road to the plantation's entrance. The plantation house is a recreation of the original built in 1935. But the row of slave cabins to the rear of the mansion dates

Visitors to Boone Hall can see what plantation life was like before the Civil War.

back some 250 years. Boone Hall gives visitors a dramatic picture of plantation life before the Civil War.

We can thank John Drayton, the quick-thinking owner of Drayton Hall, for the preservation of his lovely plantation house. In 1865, Northern troops approached Drayton Hall bent on destroying the building. But John Drayton told the soldiers the house was being used as a hospital for smallpox victims. Smallpox is a highly contagious disease, and the Northern troops fled the grounds. About 9 miles (14 km) from Charleston, Drayton Hall stands today as a splendid example of southern architecture.

Hopsewee Plantation rises along the Santee River near Georgetown. It was owned by Thomas Lynch, one of four South Carolinians who signed the Declaration of Independence. Also on the Santee River is the Hampton Plantation. One of the most impressive mansions in the state, the Hampton Plantation house boasts a marvelous portico at its entrance. That portico, or front porch, was built in 1791 to honor a very special visitor—George Washington.

Literature and the Lively Arts

As a young man, the South Carolina writer Pat Conroy taught school to impoverished black children on Daufuskie Island. He wrote about his experiences in a best-selling novel, *The Water Is Wide* (1972). Conroy also attended South Carolina's famous military college, the Citadel. He dramatized his school years in his book *The Lords of Discipline* (1980), which later became a movie. Generations of South Carolinians have created literature based on personal experiences. Mary Chestnut of Charleston wrote *A Diary*

A scene from *The Lords of Discipline*, based on Pat Conroy's novel

from Dixie (1865) during the Civil War years. Her keen observations of Southern society under the stress of war make gripping reading today. Living under cannon fire, Chestnut said of a neighboring family, "There was this poor little girl with her touchingly lovely face, and her arm gone."

South Carolinians have long excelled in folk art. Generations of black women from the lowcountry have woven baskets out of sweet grass and sold the baskets from stands. The ironwork on Charleston's old houses is so intriguing it is studied by experts from around the world. Craftspeople, unknown and unnamed, designed and built Charleston's intricate iron fences and banisters centuries ago. Wood carvings on Charleston's stately structures such as the St. Phillips Church are also a splendid expression of some folk artist. The woodworking skills needed to create such marvelous

Robert Mills

Born in Charleston in 1781, Robert Mills was perhaps the most influential architect in early U.S. history. He studied in Washington, D.C., where he was a close friend of President Thomas Jefferson. In South Carolina, he designed the state hospital for the insane, creating the first such building that was more a hospital than a prison. A fine example of Mills's work is the Robert Mills Historic House, a mansion built in Columbia in 1823. Mills built classic structures in the nation's capital such as the treasury, the post office, and the patent office. His fame endures through his masterpiece, the Washington Monument, which was for many years the world's tallest building. ■

Jasper Johns is known for his pop art style.

designs died out long ago. When church leaders decided to renovate St. Phillips woodwork in 1920, the only person they could find competent to do the job was a former slave who was in his eighties.

South Carolina's most prominent modern painter is Jasper Johns, who was born in Allendale and has lived in Edisto Beach. Johns is a leader in the pop art movement. He creates paintings of common objects such as beer cans and flashlights. In this way, Johns gives special artistic attention to things seen every day. The

South Carolina Arts Commission sponsors an apprentice program that allows talented amateurs to work under the instruction of masterful painters and sculptors. Visitors may see artists at work at Columbia's Vista Studios. The town of McCormick has a small artist's colony where painters and craftspeople work.

Catfish Row

In 1935, the composer George Gershwin wrote *Porgy and Bess*, the most popular folk opera ever produced in the United States. With a powerful musical score, Gershwin described the lives and loves within an African-American fishing community called Catfish Row.

Gershwin wrote the music while vacationing in South Carolina. His Catfish Row was inspired by a neighborhood along Church Street in Charleston. The libretto for the opera was based on the novel, *Porgy* (1925), written by the South Carolina author DuBose Heyward. ▨

Movies Shot in the Palmetto State

South Carolina is no Hollywood, but many feature films have been made in the Palmetto State. Here is a partial list:

The Abyss

Days of Thunder

Die Hard with a Vengeance

Forrest Gump

Last Dance

Paradise

The Prince of Tides

That Darn Cat (left) ■

South Carolina has music for all tastes. Active in the Palmetto State are fourteen symphony orchestras and thirty-five dance companies. The Palmetto Mastersingers, a men's chorus from Columbia, sing ballads as well as songs from Broadway musicals. Probably the best-known musical event held in the state is Charleston's Spoleto Festival held in May and June. The festival draws performers from all over the world to sing opera and lively music of all varieties. Charleston also holds an annual Low-country Blues Bash where African-American blues artists perform. A spin of the radio dial confirms that country music is loved throughout the state.

Community theater is a neighborhood or small-town institution. The theater building might be converted from a warehouse or a barn. The actors are either local people or well-traveled professionals who drive from town to town. South Carolina has seventy-seven such community theaters. The oldest community theater is the Town Theater of Columbia, founded in 1919. The small-theater tradition provides entertainment and helps to bring communities together.

Palmetto Pros

South Carolina has no professional sports franchises, but its sons and daughters have achieved stunning success in the pros:

Larry Doby (below), the first black baseball player and first black manager in the American League, was born in Camden.

Alex English, born in Columbia, was the National Basketball Association scoring champion in 1983.

Defensive lineman William "The Refrigerator" Perry (below), born in Aiken, was a key member of the Chicago Bears Super Bowl team in 1986.

Althea Gibson (right), born in the town of Silver, won the Wimbledon tennis championship in 1957 and 1958, becoming the first black player to win that title.

A tragic figure in baseball was Shoeless Joe Jackson, born in Brandon Mills in 1888. Old-time fans claimed Shoeless Joe hit line drives that were so blistering they tore the gloves off infielders. Jackson, who could barely read or write, was banned from baseball after he and several other players were convicted of fixing the outcome of the 1919 World Series. ■

Phil Mickelson playing golf at Hilton Head

Sports, Fairs, and Fun

College and high-school team sports are a major draw for Palmetto fans. High-school football and basketball games fill stadiums, especially in small towns and farm regions. The state's North-South All-Star Football Game held at the end of the year brings together South Carolina's best high-school players. College games command the loyalty of the entire state. Clemson was known for years as a football power, but in the 1990s its basketball program improved. The University of South Carolina's Fighting Gamecocks have long been a football and basketball favorite for Palmetto rooters.

Golf is played in every area of the state. There are ninety golf courses in the coastal Grand Strand region alone. The Heritage Classic Golf tournament held at Hilton Head Island is a major event. In terms of attendance, stock-car racing is the state's third most popular sport. The TranSouth 400 stock-car race held in Darlington every March is a championship contest for racing fans. Aiken, the state's horse center, hosts regular polo matches.

Medieval games and bagpipe contests are staged every September during Charleston's Scottish Games and Highland Gathering. A kid's favorite happening is the Governor's Annual Frog Jumping Contest held every spring in Springfield.

The South Carolina State Fair is the perfect place for good food and lots of fun.

Fun-loving Palmetto people need little excuse to hold a fair or a community get-together. More than 15,000 people gather every August in Saluda to watch the Young Farmers' Tractor Pull. At a bash in Waterboro, hosts cook what they claim is "the world's largest pot of rice" to celebrate the Colleton County Rice Festival. The South Carolina Peanut Party, held in the town of Pelion, boils four and a half tons of peanuts for party-goers. Square-dancing and fiddling contests are highlights of the upcountry town of Mountain Rest's Hillbilly Day. The Golden Leaf Festival, held in Mullins, has—of all things—a "Husband Hollering" contest.

Guests at these fairs are expected to gorge on food. And few people can resist the scrumptious southern cooking served in the Palmetto State. Seafood is the pride of the coastal region. Restaurants along the coast serve crabs, clam, and shrimp. Remember the state fruit—the peach—when in the upcountry. Enjoy delicious peach cobblers and peach pie. Barbecued meat and poultry are also favored in the upcountry.

Vertamae Cooks

Vertamae Grosvenor hosts a popular cooking show on public television. With pride, Vertamae says she is from "the heart of the South Carolina lowcountry." Her show is called *America's Family Kitchen*, and her book is titled *Vertamae Cooks*. She teaches amateur cooks how to make marvelous seafood creations from recipes that have been popular in her community for generations. Vertamae says that in the lowcountry, "rice is served with every meal," and she includes many mouthwatering rice dishes. ◼

South Carolinians are always welcoming visitors and tourists

Fun in South Carolina is expected of every visitor. Palmetto people are disappointed when guests fail to enjoy themselves. And few visitors fail to have a good time. South Carolina is an interesting state full of friendly people. Though it has had a rich history, its citizens welcome change.

Timeline

United States History

The first permanent British settlement is established in North America at Jamestown. **1607**

Pilgrims found Plymouth Colony, the second permanent British settlement. **1620**

America declares its independence from England. **1776**

The Treaty of Paris officially ends the Revolutionary War in America. **1783**

The U.S. Constitution is written. **1787**

The Louisiana Purchase almost doubles the size of the United States. **1803**

The United States and Britain **1812–15** fight the War of 1812.

The North and South fight **1861–65** each other in the American Civil War.

South Carolina State History

1670 English people found the first white settlement in South Carolina.

1680 English settlers found Charles Towne, the site that is now Charleston.

1703 Carolina colonists fight French and Spanish at Charles Towne during Queen Anne's War (1702–1713).

1729 British leaders divide Carolina territory into North Carolina and South Carolina.

1781 Led by General Daniel Morgan, South Carolinians fight against British soldiers at Cowpens.

1786 Columbia is chosen as the territory's capital.

1788 South Carolina officially becomes the eighth U.S. state when representatives sign the U.S. Constitution on May 23.

1832 The federal government's tax law is struck down by South Carolina.

1860 South Carolina withdraws from the Union on December 20 in opposition to Lincoln's political views.

1861 The Civil War begins when federal post Fort Sumter is attacked by South Carolina troops.

United States History

The United States is **1917–18**
involved in World War I.

The Stock market crashes, **1929**
plunging the United States into
the Great Depression.

The United States **1941–45**
fights in World War II.
The United States becomes a **1945**
charter member of the U.N.

The United States **1951–53**
fights in the Korean War.

The U.S. Congress enacts a series of **1964**
groundbreaking civil rights laws.

The United States **1964–73**
engages in the Vietnam War.

The United States and other **1991**
nations fight the brief
Persian Gulf War against Iraq.

South Carolina State History

1868 South Carolina rejoins the Union.

1877 Reconstruction ends in South Carolina.

1917–19 Many South Carolinians flock to
northern cities seeking factory jobs
during World War I (1914–1918).

1921 Boll weevils destroy much of the state's
cotton crop.

1947 Judge J. Waites Waring rules that
blacks in South Carolina may vote with
whites during primary elections.

1963 Harvey Gantt is the first black student
to attend a white university in South
Carolina

Fast Facts

The capitol

Statehood date	May 23, 1788, the 8th state
Origin of state name	Territory originally called Carolana, from *Carolus*, Latin for "Charles." The territory is later divided between North and South Carolina.
State capital	Columbia
State nickname	Palmetto State
State mottoes	*Animis Opibusque Parati* (Prepared in Mind and Resources); *Dum Spiro Spero* (While I Breathe, I Hope)
State bird	Carolina wren
State flower	Carolina jessamine, or yellow jasmine
State animal	White-tailed deer
State game bird	Wild turkey
State gem	Amethyst
State fish	Striped bass
State reptile	Loggerhead turtle
State insect	Carolina mantid

Carolina wren

Loggerhead turtle

Peach trees

State butterfly	Eastern tiger swallowtail
State dog	Boykin spaniel
State shell	Lettered olive
State fruit	Peach
State beverage	Milk
State hospitality beverage	Tea
State stone	Blue granite
State song	"Carolina"
State tree	Palmetto
State fair	Columbia (early to mid-October)
Total area; rank	31,189 sq. mi. (80,780 sq km); 40th
Land; rank	30,111 sq. mi. (77,987 sq km); 40th
Water; rank	1,078 sq. mi. (2,792 sq km); 27th
Inland water; rank	1,006 sq. mi. (2,606 sq km); 21st
Coastal water; rank	72 sq. mi. (186 sq km); 17th
Geographic center	Richland, 13 miles (21 km) southeast of Columbia
Latitude and longitude	South Carolina is approximately between 32° 04' and 35° 12' N and 78° 31' and 83° 23' W
Highest point	Sassafras Mountain, 3,560 feet (1,085 m)
Lowest point	Atlantic Ocean, sea level
Largest city	Columbia
Number of counties	46

Sassafras Mountain

Longest river	Santee River, 143 miles (230 km)
Population; rank	3,505,707 (1990 census); 25th
Density	113 persons per sq. mi. (43 per sq km)
Population distribution	55% urban, 45% rural

Ethnic distribution (does not equal 100%)

White	69.03%
African-American	29.82%
Hispanic	0.88%
Asian and Pacific Islanders	0.64%
Other	0.26%
Native American	0.24%

Santee River

Record high temperature	111° F (44°C) in Blackville on September 4, 1925; in Calhoun Falls on September 8, 1925; and in Camden on June 28, 1954
Record low temperature	−20° F (−29 °C) at Caesars Head on January 18,1977
Average July temperature	80° F (27°C)
Average January temperature	45°F (7°C)
Average annual precipitation	48 inches (122 cm)

Natural Areas and Historic Sites

National Historic Sites
Charles Pinckney Historic Site is named after the statesman who was one of the signers of the U.S. Constitution.

Francis Marion National Forest

Ninety-Six National Historic Site commemorates the site of Nathanael Greene's seige during the Revolutionary War.

National Monuments

Congaree Swamp National Monument protects the last significant stand of southern bottomland hardwood forest in the United States.

Fort Sumter National Monument commemorates the site of the first engagement in the American Civil War in 1861.

National Battlefield

Cowpens National Battlefield is the site of a decisive victory in the Revolutionary War.

National Military Park

Kings Mountain National Military Park is the site of a colonial victory over the British in 1780 during the Revolutionary War.

National Forests

Sumter National Forest lies in the northwestern part of South Carolina.

Francis Marion National Forest is in southeastern South Carolina and is named for the Revolutionary War general.

State Parks

Table Rock State Park is a scenic area of mountains and dense forests.

General Thomas Sumter Historical Site is in Stateburg and includes the gravesite of the Revolutionary War leader.

Andrew Jackson Historical State Park is in the region of the state where the U.S. president was born.

Table Rock State Park

Sports Teams

NCAA Teams (Division 1)
Charleston Southern University Buccaneers
The Citadel Bulldogs
Clemson University Tigers

Clemson basketball

Coastal Carolina University Chanticleers
College of Charleston Cougars
Furman University Paladins
South Carolina State University Bulldogs
University of South Carolina Fighting Gamecocks
Winthrop College Eagles
Wofford College Terriers

Cultural Institutions

Libraries

The Charleston Library Society, one of the first municipal libraries in America, was founded in 1748 and is still in operation.

The State Library (Columbia) is housed in the Department of Archives and History.

Museums

The South Carolina State Museum (Columbia) contains the work of South Carolina artists as well as exhibits on science and industry.

The Charleston Museum houses a collection of South Carolina memorabilia.

The Gibbes Art Gallery of the Carolina Art Association (Charleston); the *Columbia Museum of Art*; the *Florence Museum of Art, Science, and History*; and the *Greenville County Museum of Art* all have collections of fine art.

Performing Arts

South Carolina has fourteen symphony orchestras, thirty-five dance companies, and one major opera company.

Universities and Colleges

In the mid-1990s, South Carolina had thirty-four public and twenty-eight private institutions of higher learning.

University of South Carolina

Brookgreen Gardens

Annual Events

January–March

Oyster Festival in Charleston (early February)

Polo Games in Aiken (March to June)

Garden Tours, statewide (February–May)

Canadian-American Days at Myrtle Beach (mid-March)

TranSouth Financial 400 stock-car race in Darlington (late March)

Plantation Tours, throughout the state (March–April)

April–June

The Governor's Annual Frog Jumping Contest in Springfield (Saturday before Easter)

MCI Classic golf tournament at Hilton Head Island (April)

Blessing of the Fleet and Seafood Festival in Mount Pleasant (late April)

Pontiac's Freedom Weekend Aloft in Greenville (late May)

Gullah Cultural Festival in Beaufort (late May)

Iris Festival in Sumter (late May)

Spoleto Festival U.S.A. in Charleston (May–June)

Sun-Fun Festival in Myrtle Beach (June)

July–September

Peach Festival in Gaffney (early July)

Little Mountain Reunion in Little Mountain (first Saturday in August)

Southern 500 stock-car race in Darlington (Sunday before Labor Day)

Scottish Games and Highland Gathering at Middleton Place Gardens near Charleston (mid-September)

October–December

State Fair in Columbia (early to mid-October)

Colonial Cup in Camden (November)

Chitlin Strut in Salley (Saturday after Thanksgiving)

Charleston

State fair

Famous People

Bernard Baruch (1870–1965)	Statesman, philanthropist, and financier
Mary McLeod Bethune (1875–1955)	Educator
James Francis Byrnes (1879–1972)	Supreme Court justice
John Caldwell Calhoun (1782–1850)	Public official and political leader
Thomas Green Clemson (1807–1888)	Engineer and educator
Pat Conroy (1945–)	Writer
James Dickey (1923–1997)	Poet and writer
Charles Fraser (1782–1860)	Artist
Althea Gibson (1927–)	Tennis player
John "Dizzy" Gillespie (1917–1993)	Jazz trumpet player
Angelina Emily Grimké (1805–1879) and Sara Moore Grimké (1792–1873)	Abolitionists and supporters of women's rights
Edwin Heywood (1885–1940)	Poet and author
Thomas Heywood (1746–1809)	Soldier, patriot, politician
Ernest "Fritz" Hollings (1922–)	Politician
Josephine Humphreys (1945–)	Author
Andrew Jackson (1767–1845)	U.S. president
Jesse Jackson (1941–)	Minister and civil rights leader
Lane Kirkland (1922–)	Labor leader
Eartha Kitt (1928–)	Singer and actor
Henry Laurens (1724–1792)	Political leader
James Longstreet (1821–1904)	Confederate general
Andie MacDowell (1958–)	Actor

Jesse Jackson

Francis "Swamp Fox" Marion (1732?–1795)	Revolutionary soldier
Andrew Pinckney (1739–1817)	Statesman
Charles Pinckney (1757–1824)	Statesman
Charles Cotesworth Pinckney (1746–1825)	Statesman
Thomas Pinckney (1750–1828)	Statesman
Joel Roberts Poinsett (1779–1851)	Diplomat
Mickey Spillane (1918–)	Novelist
James "Strom" Thurmond (1902–)	Politician

Strom Thurmond

To Find Out More

History

- Fradin, Dennis Brindell. *South Carolina*. Chicago: Childrens Press, 1992.

- Fradin, Dennis Brindell. *The South Carolina Colony*. Chicago: Childrens Press, 1992.

- Fredeen, Charles. *South Carolina*. Minneapolis: Lerner, 1992.

- January, Brendan. *Fort Sumter*. Danbury, Conn.: Children's Press, 1997.

- Russell, Ching Yeung. *A Day on a Shrimp Boat*. Columbia, S.C.: Sandlapper Publishing Co., 1993.

- Thompson, Kathleen. *South Carolina*. Austin, Tex.: Raintree/Steck Vaughn, 1996.

Biographies

- Anderson, Levere. *Mary McLeod Bethune*. Broomall, Penn.: Chelsea House, 1991.

- Brown, Warren. *John C. Calhoun*. Broomall, Penn.: Chelsea House, 1993.

- Gentry, Tony. *Dizzie Gillespie*. Broomall, Penn.: Chelsea House, 1994.

- Lyons, Mary E., and Mannie Garcia (illus.). *Catching the Fire: Philip Simmons, Blacksmith*. New York: Houghton Mifflin, 1997.

- Simon, Charnan. *Jesse Jackson: I Am Somebody*. Danbury, Conn.: Children's Press, 1997.

Fiction

- Houston, Gloria. *Will: A Sunny Land with a Sunny Brook*. New York: Putnam, 1995.

- Kovach, Gay Haff. *Ghost in the Capitol*. Columbia, S.C.: Sandlapper Publishing Co., 1986.

Websites

- **State of South Carolina**
  http://www.state.sc.us/
  Official website for South Carolina state government

- **South Carolina Institute of Archaeology and Anthropology**
  http://www.cla.sc.edu/sciaa/sciaa.html
  Concerned with preserving South Carolina's prehistoric and historic culture

Addresses

- **Division of Tourism**
  P.O. Box 71
  Columbia, SC 29202
  For information about travel and tourism in South Carolina

- **South Carolina Department of Archives and History**
  P.O. Box 11669
  1430 Senate Street
  Columbia, SC 29211
  For information about South Carolina's history

Index

Page numbers in *italics* indicate illustrations.

Meet the Author

I'm R. Conrad Stein. I was born and grew up in Chicago. I lived in a not very prosperous neighborhood on the city's North Side. At an early age (seventeen years) I joined the Marine Corps. Later I attended the University of Illinois, where I graduated with a degree in history. I now live in Chicago with my wife, Deborah Kent, and our daughter, Janna. I earn my living writing history and geography books for young readers. Over the years I have published more than eighty books for various companies.

How do I write books on American states or on foreign countries? First of all, I visit the place I'm writing about and talk to the people. This was easy in the case of South Carolina because residents there are so friendly and outgoing. Then I contact government agencies and get the latest figures on population, industrial development, and the like. I read the history of the state. I especially like to probe into the diaries of early travelers and pioneers. Finally, I make an outline covering the points I wish to make. Then comes the work—I sit down and write.

It's not all work, however, since writing allows me to travel and read. As a kid I loved to look at maps and to study people living in distant lands. Because my family couldn't afford to travel, I grew up looking at a place like the state of Minnesota as an exotic land because it was so far away from the North Side of Chicago. Now I travel often, but I still enjoy reading—and writing—about other places and the people living in those places.

Photo Credits